KIDS' BIBLE ACTIVITIES

Vickie Save
Illustrated by Ken Save

BARBOUR
PUBLISHING

Published by Barbour Publishing, Inc., P.O. Box 719, Uhrichsville, Ohio 44683, www.barbourbooks.com

Our mission is to publish and distribute inspirational products offering exceptional value and biblical encouragement to the masses.

ecpa Member of the
Evangelical Christian
Publishers Association

Printed in the United States of America.
5 4 3 2 1

FIND THE WORDS BELOW IN THE WORD SEARCH PUZZLE.

```
J R U A M D C I W A U I H X
M G O T P N S C S M L E I J
I O E B F T L O V E D Y M G
E D R K T B J F C V T G H K
Q L Q O S E H Q P B N I P L
E A D B E L I E V E S D M T
C H R X W B S C O G K O L Q
L W O R L D A S U D U F B W
W R Q G U H O A M V K L A J
I N B S D T Y N P W A I C Z
P K L Y V L O D U X Z F O S
Z P E R I S H B N V T E K V
H F I J G F Y X H C W B H F
P E T E R N A L T O B G Q J
D N R J G Z M E X Y N V R Z
```

ETERNAL   HIM

WORLD   LIFE

SON   BELIEVES

PERISH   HIS

GOD   LOVED

3

"FOR GOD SO LOVED THE WORLD..."

4   FINISH THE PICTURE.

FIND THE WORDS TO THIS VERSE IN THE WORDSEARCH BELOW.

"FOR ALL HAVE SINNED AND FALL SHORT OF THE GLORY OF GOD."

ROMANS 3:23

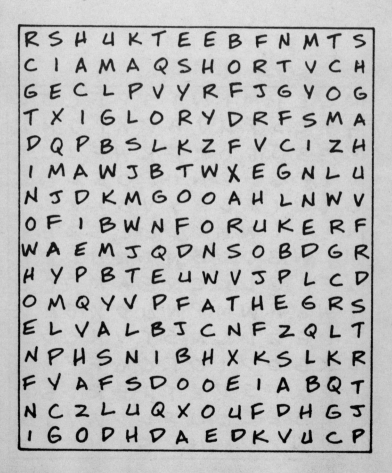

```
R S H U K T E E B F N M T S
C I A M A Q S H O R T V C H
G E C L P V Y R F J G Y O G
T X I G L O R Y D R F S M A
D Q P B S L K Z F V C I Z H
I M A W J B T W X E G N L U
N J D K M G O O A H L N W V
O F I B W N F O R U K E R F
W A E M J Q D N S O B D G R
H Y P B T U W V J P L C D
O M Q Y V P F A T H E G R S
E L V A L B J C N F Z Q L T
N P H S N I B H X K S L K R
F Y A F S D O O E I A B Q T
N C Z L U Q X O U F D H G J
I G O D H D A E D K V U C P
```

5

FIND THE WORDS TO THIS VERSE
IN THE WORDSEARCH BELOW.

"...WHILE WE WERE STILL SINNERS,
CHRIST DIED FOR US."

ROMANS 5:8b

USE THE CODE CHART TO MATCH THE
NUMBERS WITH LETTERS. USE THE
COLUMN GOING DOWN, FIRST, THEN
WRITE THE LETTERS IN THE BLANKS.

	1	2	3	4	5	6
1	A	F	K	P	U	Z
2	B	G	L	Q	V	
3	C	H	M	R	W	
4	D	I	N	S	X	
5	E	J	O	T	Y	

"

12 53 34   54 32 51   35 11 22 51 44   53 12

44 42 43   42 44   41 51 11 54 32 ,   21 15 54

54 32 51   22 42 12 54   53 12   22 53 41

42 44   51 54 51 34 43 11 23   23 42 12 51

42 43   31 32 34 42 44 54   52 51 44 15 44

"

53 15 34   23 53 34 41 .

ROMANS 6:23   7

CONNECT-THE-DOTS

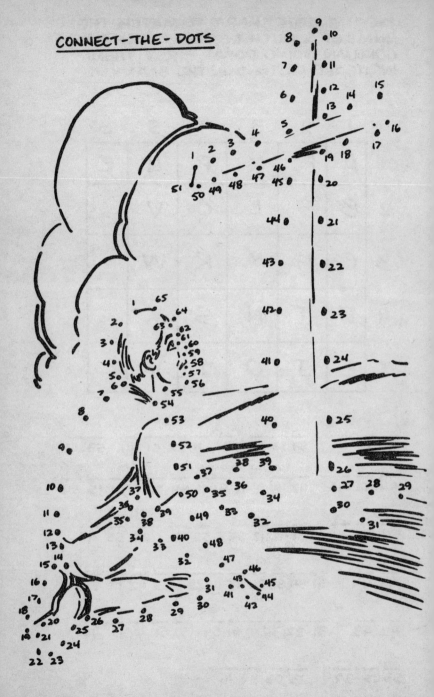

8

TRAVEL THE PATH THAT MAKES A SENTENCE.

START

I AM THE GOING TO THE CITY

WAY AND D THE TRUTH AND

AND IN TH THOSE WHO K AND THE LIFE. NO ONE

DISCIPLES COMES TO THE

IS

BUT A VAPOUR

HE A TRUTH O W

RE

BE STILL ONE NO ONE CAN COME

COMES IN N I N G BUT THE

GI

NO ONE COMES TO THE FATHER GRACE OF

NING

GOD AND FA T H E R

YOU MUST BE BORN

F

FATHER EXCEPT THROUGH ME.

END

9

JOHN 14:6

AFTER GOING THROUGH THE MAZE ON
THE PREVIOUS PAGE, FILL IN THE BLANKS
BELOW TO FINISH THE SENTENCE.

" I __ THE ____ AND THE
_____ AND THE ____.
NO ___ _____ TO
THE _____ EXCEPT
_____ __."

JOHN 14:6

NOW FIND THE UNDERLINED WORDS IN
THE WORDSEARCH BELOW.

```
I N U L F M K O V D K Q B R
X A J E B G T Y P L P M F W
B F T R U T H U T A F E J S
A S P L Z X R D J O K H F Q
N M I C A F O R C L C B V N
U T P O B Z U O I X I T D B
V D V M R W G E O Z A F R H
H W F E L I H B Y W B G E J
K A T S S F H M C Q Y N Q M
B Y E N C E N P H L O B Z T
Y W X F A T H E R G S U F G
```

USE THE CODE CHART TO MATCH THE
NUMBERS WITH LETTERS. USE THE
COLUMN GOING DOWN, FIRST, THEN
WRITE THE LETTERS IN THE BLANKS.

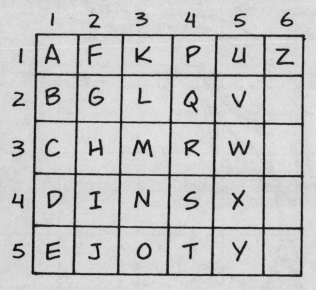

	1	2	3	4	5	6
1	A	F	K	P	U	Z
2	B	G	L	Q	V	
3	C	H	M	R	W	
4	D	I	N	S	X	
5	E	J	O	T	Y	

JOHN 5:24a

"

42 54 51 23 23 55 53 15 54 32 51

54 34 15 54 32 ' 35 32 53 51 25 51 34

32 51 11 34 44 33 55 35 53 34 41

11 43 41 21 51 23 42 51 25 51 44

32 42 33 35 32 53 44 51 43 54 33 51

32 11 44 51 54 51 34 43 11 23

23 42 12 51 11 43 41 35 42 23 23 43 53 54 "

21 51 31 53 43 41 51 33 43 51 41 ..."

FINISH THE PICTURE OF JESUS.

12

TRAVEL THE PATH THAT MAKES A SENTENCE.

START

IF YOU CONFESS WITH YOUR MOUTH THAT JESUS IS LORD AND BELIEVE IN YOUR HEART THAT GOD RAISED HIM FROM THE DEAD YOU WILL BE SAVED.

END

13

ROMANS 10:9

AFTER GOING THROUGH THE MAZE ON
THE PREVIOUS PAGE, FILL IN THE BLANKS
BELOW TO FINISH THE SENTENCE.

" IF YOU _ _ _ _ _ _ _
WITH YOUR _ _ _ _ _ _ ,
' _ _ _ _ _ _ IS _ _ _ _ ', AND
_ _ _ _ _ _ _ _ IN YOUR
_ _ _ _ _ _ THAT GOD
_ _ _ _ _ _ HIM FROM
THE _ _ _ _ , YOU WILL BE
_ _ _ _ _ . "

ROMANS 10:9

14

FIND THE WORDS BELOW IN THE WORDSEARCH PUZZLE.

```
I O E B F T L B C E S Y M G
E D M K T B J F C U T G H K
Q L O D S E B Q S B N I E L
E A U B A L T E V S E D A T
C H T X V B J C L G K O R Q
L W H R E D A S U I U F T W
W R Q G D H O A M V E L A J
I D B S D T Y N P W A V C Z
P K E Y V C O N F E S S E B
Z P E A L S H B N V T E K V
H L O R D F Y X H C W B H F
P E R V E L A R A I S E D J
D N R J G Z M E X Y N V R Z
```

LORD   RAISED

HEART   MOUTH

DEAD   BELIEVE

CONFESS   JESUS

SAVED   15

COLOR THE PICTURE.

JESUS IS KNOCKING AT THE DOOR OF YOUR HEART. WHAT SHOULD YOU DO?

USE THE CODE CHART BELOW TO MATCH THE CODES WITH LETTERS. USE THE COLUMN GOING DOWN FIRST. THEN WRITE THE LETTERS IN THE BLANKS TO COMPLETE THE VERSE.

THEN YOU WILL KNOW WHAT TO DO!

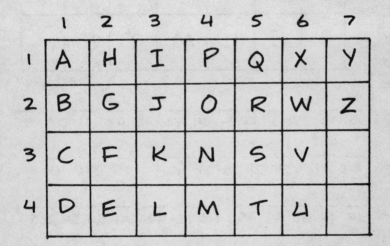

	1	2	3	4	5	6	7
1	A	H	I	P	Q	X	Y
2	B	G	J	O	R	W	Z
3	C	F	K	N	S	V	
4	D	E	L	M	T	U	

"
‾‾ ‾‾ ‾‾ ‾‾ ‾‾ ‾‾ ‾‾ !   ‾‾ ‾‾ ‾‾ ‾‾ ‾‾ ‾‾
12 42 25 42 13 11 44   13 35 45 11 34 41

‾‾ ‾‾ ‾‾ ‾‾ ‾‾ ‾‾ ‾‾ ‾‾ ‾‾   ‾‾ ‾‾ ‾‾
11 45 45 12 42 41 24 24 25   11 34 41

‾‾ ‾‾ ‾‾ ‾‾ ‾‾ "
33 34 24 31 33

CONTINUED NEXT PAGE...

	1	2	3	4	5	6	7
1	A	H	I	P	Q	X	Y
2	B	G	J	O	R	W	Z
3	C	F	K	N	S	V	
4	D	E	L	M	T	U	

"
$\overline{13}$ $\overline{32}$ $\overline{11}$ $\overline{34}$ $\overline{17}$ $\overline{24}$ $\overline{34}$ $\overline{42}$ $\overline{12}$ $\overline{42}$ $\overline{11}$ $\overline{25}$ $\overline{35}$

$\overline{44}$ $\overline{17}$ $\overline{36}$ $\overline{24}$ $\overline{13}$ $\overline{31}$ $\overline{42}$ $\overline{11}$ $\overline{34}$ $\overline{41}$

$\overline{24}$ $\overline{14}$ $\overline{42}$ $\overline{34}$ $\overline{35}$ $\overline{45}$ $\overline{12}$ $\overline{42}$ $\overline{41}$ $\overline{24}$ $\overline{24}$ $\overline{25}$,

$\overline{13}$ $\overline{26}$ $\overline{13}$ $\overline{43}$ $\overline{43}$ $\overline{31}$ $\overline{24}$ $\overline{44}$ $\overline{42}$ $\overline{13}$ $\overline{34}$

$\overline{11}$ $\overline{34}$ $\overline{41}$ $\overline{42}$ $\overline{11}$ $\overline{45}$ $\overline{26}$ $\overline{13}$ $\overline{45}$ $\overline{12}$

$\overline{12}$ $\overline{13}$ $\overline{44}$, $\overline{11}$ $\overline{34}$ $\overline{41}$ $\overline{12}$ $\overline{42}$ $\overline{26}$ $\overline{13}$ $\overline{45}$ $\overline{12}$

$\overline{44}$ $\overline{42}$. "

REVELATION 3:20

18

19

DO YOU KNOW JESUS LOVES YOU? DO YOU KNOW HOW MUCH JESUS LOVES YOU? HE LOVES YOU SO MUCH THAT HE DIED TO PAY THE PRICE FOR YOUR SIN. THERE IS ONLY ONE SIN THAT GOD WILL NOT FORGIVE. THAT SIN IS NOT BELIEVING IN JESUS AND WHAT HE DID FOR YOU AND ALL OF US. WITHOUT JESUS, WITHOUT ACCEPTING THAT HE DIED FOR US, NO ONE CAN GO TO HEAVEN.

THREE DAYS AFTER JESUS DIED, HE WAS RAISED TO NEW LIFE. HE WANTS TO SHARE THAT WITH US TOO! HE WANTS TO GIVE US NEW LIFE ... ETERNAL LIFE!

DO YOU WANT TO ASK JESUS TO COME INTO YOUR HEART AND YOUR LIFE? ALL YOU NEED TO DO IS ASK HIM. YOU COULD SAY A PRAYER LIKE THIS:

DEAR JESUS,

I KNOW I AM A SINNER AND THAT YOU DIED FOR ALL MY SINS. I KNOW YOU ROSE FROM THE DEAD. JESUS, I ASK YOU NOW TO COME INTO MY HEART AND TAKE CONTROL OF MY LIFE.
THANK YOU FOR ALL YOU HAVE DONE FOR ME.
TEACH ME YOUR WAYS, JESUS, AND HELP ME TO GROW UP WITH YOU.

IN JESUS' NAME, I PRAY. AMEN.

IF YOU HAVE NEVER INVITED JESUS INTO YOUR HEART AND LIFE BUT YOU WANT TO NOW, GO TO THE NEXT PAGE AND WRITE OUT YOUR PRAYER IN YOUR OWN WORDS. JUST TELL JESUS HOW YOU REALLY FEEL.

MY VERY OWN PRAYER TO INVITE
JESUS INTO MY HEART AND LIFE.

DATE : _____

DEAR LORD JESUS,

_____

_____

_____

_____

_____

_____

_____

_____

_____

_____

IN JESUS' NAME, AMEN.

_____
YOUR NAME

21

DID YOU INVITE JESUS INTO YOUR HEART?

FIND YOUR WAY TO JESUS:

WOW! IF YOU ASKED JESUS INTO YOUR LIFE, YOU ARE NOW A CHRISTIAN! YOU ARE NOW A CHILD OF GOD!

LET'S LEARN HOW TO GET TO KNOW JESUS BETTER.

UNSCRAMBLE THE WORDS BELOW TO FIND OUT HOW TO BEGIN.

1.) TO BECOME A CHILD OF GOD, YOU HAD TO ASK JESUS INTO YOUR HEART. THIS IS CALLED _____ .
IYGNRAP

2.) PRAYING IS _____ WITH GOD.
GTINALK

3.) JUST LIKE YOU TALK WITH YOUR MOM OR DAD, GOD_____ YOU TO ____ WITH HIM.   TWNAS   KTLA

4.) IT DOES NOT STOP THERE. GOD WANTS TO TALK TO YOU! JESUS SPEAKS TO YOU THROUGH HIS _____ .
DRWO

5.) THE ONLY WAY TO REALLY KNOW JESUS IS TO_____ ABOUT ____ .
ARDE   IMH

6.) YOU READ ABOUT _____ IN THE HOLY _____ .   JSSUE
EBLIB

IN THE FOLLOWING WORDSEARCH PUZZLE,
FIND AND CIRCLE THE WORDS LISTED.

THEY CAN BE FOUND IN LINES GOING
FORWARD, BACKWARD, UP, DOWN, OR
DIAGONALLY.

```
D F C L P V Y R F H G V O G
O X S R A E H Y D R I S M A
O Q P B S L K Z F V C M Z H
R M B W J B E A T H G N L V
N J D K M N Q O A H L N W O
O F I B O N F O D U K R P I
W A E Y J Q D N S N B D G C
H K N O C K U W V J A L C E
O A Q Y V P F A T P B T R S
V L E A L B D E V O L Q S T
```

LOVED	HEARS	EAT
KNOCK	VOICE	ANYONE
DOOR	HIM	STAND

WHAT HAVE YOU LEARNED ABOUT BEING A CHILD OF GOD?

FIND AND CIRCLE THE WORDS LISTED BELOW.

```
T X I G D O R Y D R F S M A
D Q P R S L K Z F V C I K H
I M O W J B T W X R G N L U
N W D K M G O O U H L N A V
B F I B W N G D N U R K T F
W I E M J B I B L E B D G R
H N P B T V U W V J D L C D
O V Q Y A R P A T H A G R S
H I W S L B J S U S E J L T
N T H S N I B H X K R L K R
F E F A S D O S E A I B Q T
N C Z L U Q X O U F D H G J
I G O D H D A E D K V U C P
```

PRAY   WORD   TALK

READ   JESUS   GOD

BIBLE   SAVIOUR   INVITE

25

CONNECT THE DOTS
AND FINISH THE PHRASE.

JESUS, THE _ _ _ _ _ OF JUDAH !

ACROSS

1. GOD <u>EAVG</u> US HIS ONE AND ONLY SON.

2. NOW WE CAN HAVE ETERNAL <u>FILE</u>.

3. JESUS KNOCKS AT THE DOORS OF OUR <u>TARHES</u>

4. IF WE HAVE <u>TIVDEIN</u> HIM IN, HE WILL NEVER LEAVE US.

DOWN

5. WE ARE NOW A CHILD OF <u>ODG</u>.

6. WE TALK TO HIM BY <u>YRANIGP</u>.

7. HE TALKS TO US THROUGH <u>SHI</u> WORD.

8. HIS WORD IS THE <u>BBEIL</u>.

<u>WORD LIST</u>

PRAYING	HEARTS
LIFE	BIBLE
GAVE	HIS
INVITED	GOD

28

SOMETIMES, IT'S NOT EASY TO READ THE
BIBLE EVERY DAY. OTHER *THINGS*
WILL TRY TO GET IN THE WAY, BUT IF YOU
REALLY WANT TO GROW AS A CHRISTIAN, IT IS
BEST TO READ IN GOD'S WORD EACH DAY.

FIND YOUR WAY TO THE BIBLE.

TRAVEL THE PATH THAT MAKES A SENTENCE.

START

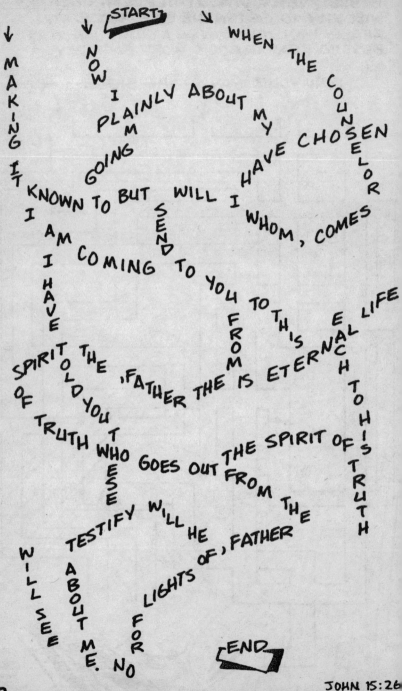

When the Counselor whom, I have chosen, comes to this, Eternal life each to his truth, the spirit of, Father lights of, father from the spirit of, who goes out these truth of, spirit the, old you told, Father the is, from to you send, but will, known to, it am coming, I have, I am, going, I am, now, making it, will he testify, will about me. no, for, will see.

END

30

JOHN 15:26

AFTER GOING THROUGH THE MAZE ON THE PREVIOUS PAGE, FILL IN THE BLANKS BELOW TO FINISH THE SENTENCE.

"WHEN THE _ _ _ _ _ _ _ _ _ _ _
COMES, _ _ _ _ I WILL
_ _ _ _ TO _ _ _ FROM THE
_ _ _ _ _ _ , THE _ _ _ _ _ _
OF _ _ _ _ _ _ WHO _ _ _ _
OUT FROM THE FATHER, HE
WILL _ _ _ _ _ _ _
_ _ _ _ _ ME."

JOHN 15:26

31

FIND THE WORDS BELOW IN THE WORDSEARCH PUZZLE.

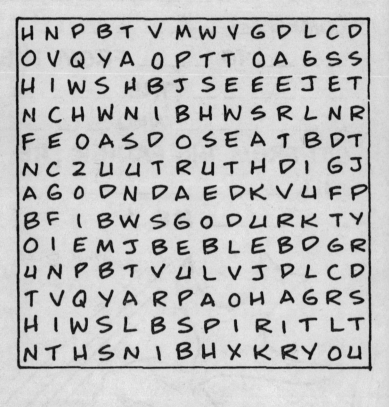

```
H N P B T V M W V G D L C D
O V Q Y A O P T T O A G S S
H I W S H B J S E E E J E T
N C H W N I B H W S R L N R
F E O A S D O S E A T B D T
N C Z U U T R U T H D I G J
A G O D N D A E D K V U F P
B F I B W S G O D U R K T Y
O I E M J B E B L E B D G R
U N P B T V U L V J D L C D
T V Q Y A R P A O H A G R S
H I W S L B S P I R I T L T
N T H S N I B H X K R Y O U
```

SPIRIT   WHOM   YOU

ABOUT   TRUTH   TESTIFY

GOES   COUNSELOR   SEND

COLOR THE PICTURE

WHEN YOU BECOME A CHILD OF GOD, WHERE DOES THE HOLY SPIRIT LIVE?

GO ON TO THE NEXT PAGE TO FIND THE ANSWER.

USE THE CODE CHART BELOW TO MATCH THE CODES WITH LETTERS. USE THE COLUMN GOING DOWN, FIRST, THEN WRITE THE LETTERS IN THE BLANKS.

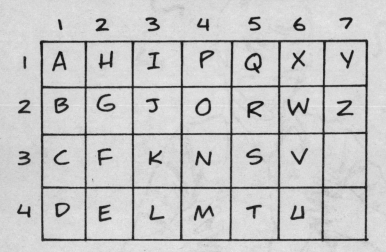

	1	2	3	4	5	6	7
1	A	H	I	P	Q	X	Y
2	B	G	J	O	R	W	Z
3	C	F	K	N	S	V	
4	D	E	L	M	T	U	

"

__ __ __ __ __ __ __ __ __ __ __ __
41 24 17 24 46 34 24 45 33 34 24 26

__ __ __ __ __ __ __ __ __ __ __ __
45 12 11 45 17 24 46 25 21 24 41 17

__ __ __ __ __ __ __ __ __ __ __
13 35 11 45 42 44 14 43 42 24 32

__ __ __ __ __ __ __ __ __ __ __ __ __ ⁷
45 12 42 12 24 43 17 35 14 13 25 13 45

__ __ __ __ __ __ __ __ __ __ ⁷
26 12 24 13 35 13 34 17 24 46

__ __ __ __ __ __ __ __ __ __ __
26 12 24 44 17 24 46 12 11 36 42

__ __ __ __ __ __ __ __ __ __ __ __ __ __ __ ?"
25 42 31 42 13 36 42 41 32 25 24 44 22 24 41

1 CORINTHIANS 6:19

THE HOLY SPIRIT ACTUALLY COMES TO
LIVE INSIDE YOU! YOUR BODY BECOMES
THE TEMPLE, OR DWELLING PLACE, OF GOD'S
SPIRIT.

THIS IS HARD TO UNDERSTAND BECAUSE
WE CAN'T SEE HIM, BUT IT IS TRUE BECAUSE
THE BIBLE SAYS IT IS SO. MANY TIMES
THE HOLY SPIRIT MAKES HIS PRESENCE
KNOWN. WE CAN FEEL HIM AS HE GIVES
US HIS POWER AND STRENGTH TO LIVE
AS GOD WANTS US TO LIVE.

CONNECT-THE-DOTS

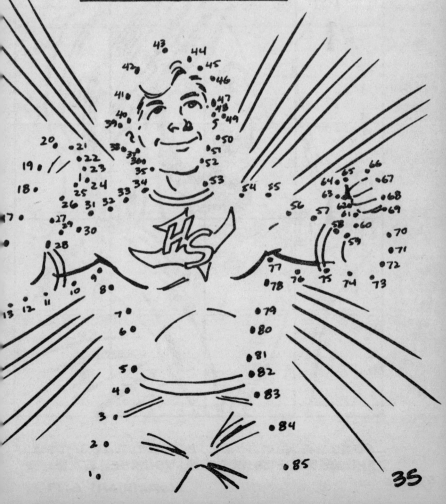

35

ONCE, OUR HUMAN SPIRITS WERE DEAD. WE WERE BORN SPIRITUALLY DEAD. JESUS GIVES US NEW LIFE IN OUR SPIRITS!

"FOR JUST AS THE FATHER RAISES THE DEAD AND GIVES THEM LIFE, EVEN SO THE SON GIVES LIFE TO WHOM HE IS PLEASED TO GIVE IT."

JOHN 5:21

GO TO THE NEXT PAGE. USING THE GRID, DRAW THE ABOVE PICTURE FOR YOURSELF.

FROM THE PREVIOUS PAGE, USE THE
GRID TO DRAW THE PICTURE FOR YOURSELF.

NOW THAT YOU ARE A CHRISTIAN, YOU MUST LET THE HOLY SPIRIT TEACH YOU HOW TO LIVE YOUR NEW LIFE. HOW DOES HE DO THIS?

USE THE CODE CHART BELOW TO MATCH THE CODES WITH LETTERS. USE THE COLUMN GOING DOWN, FIRST, THEN WRITE THE LETTERS IN THE BLANKS ON THE FOLLOWING PAGE.

	1	2	3	4	5	6	7
1	A	B	C	D	E	F	G
2	H	I	J	K	L	M	N
3	O	P	Q	R	S	T	U
4	V	W	X	Y	Z		

WHAT YOU PUT INTO YOUR MIND, WHAT YOU READ OR WATCH OR LISTEN TO, IS WHAT WILL COME OUT OF YOU. IF YOU PUT GOD'S WORD IN, IF YOU READ THE BIBLE REGULARLY, GOD'S CHARACTER WILL COME OUT OF YOU IN THE WAYS YOU THINK, ACT AND THE CHOICES YOU MAKE.

USING THE CODE CHART FROM THE
PREVIOUS PAGE, COMPLETE THE VERSE
BELOW.

"
___ ___   ___ ___ ___   ___ ___ ___   ___ ___ ___ ___
14 31   27 31 36   13 31 27   16 31 34 26

___ ___ ___   ___ ___ ___ ___ ___ ___   ___ ___ ___ ___ ___
11 27 44   25 31 27 17 15 34   36 31 36 21 15

___ ___ ___ ___ ___ ___ ___   ___ ___   ___ ___ ___ ___
32 11 36 36 15 34 27   31 16   36 21 22 35

___ ___ ___ ___ ___ ,   ___ ___ ___   ___ ___
42 31 34 25 14   12 37 36   12 15

___ ___ ___ ___ ___ ___ ___ ___ ___ ___ ___   ___ ___
36 34 11 27 35 16 31 34 26 15 14   12 44

___ ___ ___   ___ ___ ___ ___ ___ ___ ___ ___   ___
36 21 15   34 15 27 15 42 22 27 17   17

___ ___   ___ ___ ___ ___   ___ ___ ___ ___ .   "
31 16   44 31 37 34   26 22 27 14

ROMANS 12:2

COLOR THE PICTURE

BE CAREFUL IN YOUR CHOICES!

TRAVEL THE PATH THAT MAKES A SENTENCE.

START

DO NOT

ANYONE WHO

BUT

THE FRUIT OF

USE YOUR

LOVE JOY PEACE

THE SPIRIT IS

RECEIVES

LET US

FULNESS GOODNESS KINDNESS PATIENCE

THOSE WHO WANT

OF

TO MAKE A

BE

NOT

COME

LET US

BROTHER

GROW WEARY

AND

THE PEACE

NESS

WERE AND MERCY TO

ALL WHO

NOT

BECOME

SELF-CONTROL.

ED TO BE

END

41

GALATIANS 5:22-23a

AFTER GOING THROUGH THE MAZE ON
THE PREVIOUS PAGE, FILL IN THE
BLANKS BELOW TO FINISH THE VERSE.

"BUT THE _ _ _ _ _ OF
THE _ _ _ _ _ _ IS

_ _ _ _ , _ _ _ _ ,

_ _ _ _ _ ,

_ _ _ _ _ _ _ _ ,

_ _ _ _ _ _ _ ,

_ _ _ _ _ _ _ ,

_ _ _ _ _ _ _ _ _ ,

_ _ _ _ _ _ _ _

AND _ _ _ _ - _ _ _ _ _ _

GALATIANS 5:22-23 a

FIND THE WORDS BELOW IN THE
WORDSEARCH PUZZLE.

```
P F O S P I R I T A J B D G
N A Z U E T R U T H O I G O
A I T K N L A E D K Y U F O
B T I I W S F R U I T K T D
O H E N E B E C L E B D G N
U F P D T N U L O J D L C E
A U O N N D C E D N V U F S
B L I E W S G E D U T K T S
C N E S J B E L B B E R G R
H E W S L B S P I C L T O T
N S H S N I B H A K R O O L
T S G E N T L E N E S S V S
H I W S L B P P I D T I L E
```

JOY   KINDNESS

SELF-CONTROL   SPIRIT

GENTLENESS   PATIENCE

PEACE   GOODNESS

FRUIT   LOVE

FAITHFULNESS   43

THE FRUIT OF THE SPIRIT

FILL IN THE BLANKS.

P _ _ _ _ N _ _

_ _ O _ N _ S _

L _ _ E

F _ _ _ H _ _ N _ _ _ _

L - _ N _ _ L

_ _ A _ _

K _ _ D _ _ S _

_ _ _ Y

_ _ N _ E _ E _ _

YOU ALREADY KNOW THAT WHEN YOU
BECOME A CHRISTIAN, THE HOLY SPIRIT
COMES TO LIVE IN YOU. THE HOLY SPIRIT
WILL LEAD YOU INTO GOD'S TRUTH, AND
HE WILL DO THE WORK OF PRODUCING
GOD'S CHARACTER IN YOU, IF YOU WILL
LET HIM. YOU CAN DO THAT BY CHOOSING
TO DO WHAT GOD WANTS RATHER THAN
WHAT YOU WANT. THIS IS CALLED
SURRENDERING, OR GIVING UP, TO GOD'S
WILL.

GOD'S CHARACTER IS THE FRUIT OF
THE SPIRIT.

UNSCRAMBLE THE WORDS BELOW TO
FIND GOD'S CHARACTER, THE FRUIT OF
THE SPIRIT.

OVLE　　　　　　— — — —

OYJ　　　　　　　— — —

PCEEA　　　　　— — — — —

TIEENCPA　　　— — — — — — — —

DNNESKSI　　　— — — — — — — —

OGDOSSNE　　　— — — — — — — —

HTAIFLUNFSES

　　　　— — — — — — — — — —

TNLEEEGSSN

　　　　　— — — — — — — — —

- RTNSFLEOCLO

　　　— — — — - — — — — — — —

FIND YOUR WAY THROUGH THE
OBSTACLES, THE THINGS OF THIS WORLD,
THAT WILL TRY TO PULL YOU AWAY FROM
WHAT GOD WOULD WANT YOU TO DO.

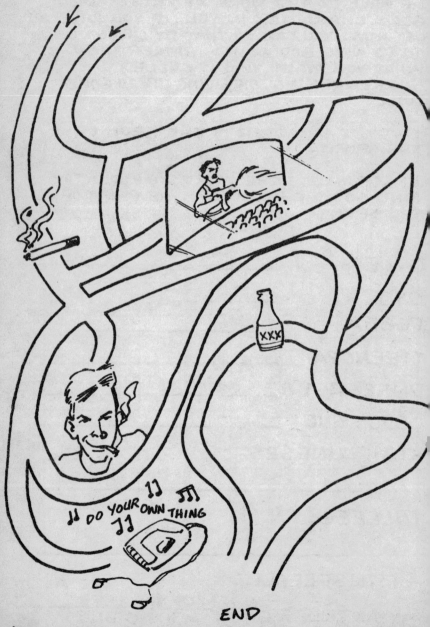

END

FINISH THE PICTURE

AS YOU START TO LIVE YOUR NEW LIFE AS GOD'S CHILD, IT IS IMPORTANT TO KNOW WHO YOUR ENEMIES ARE !

THE CHRISTIAN HAS THREE ENEMIES :
   1. THE DEVIL
   2. THE SINFUL NATURE (THE FLESH)
   3. THE WORLD

A CHRISTIAN IN THIS WORLD IS LIKE A SOLDIER — A SOLDIER OF THE LORD. YOUR ONLY WEAPON IS THE BIBLE.

USE THE CODE CHART BELOW TO MATCH
THE CODES WITH LETTERS. USE THE
COLUMN GOING DOWN, FIRST, THEN
WRITE THE LETTERS IN THE BLANKS.

	1	2	3	4	5	6	7
1	A	B	C	D	E	F	G
2	H	I	J	K	L	M	N
3	O	P	Q	R	S	T	U
4	V	W	X	Y	Z		

"

‾‾ ‾‾   ‾‾ ‾‾ ‾‾ ‾‾   ‾‾ ‾‾ ‾‾ ‾‾ ‾‾ ‾‾ ‾‾ ‾‾ ‾‾ ‾
12 15   35 15 25 16   13 31 27 36 34 31 25 25 15 1

‾‾ ‾‾ ‾‾   ‾‾ ‾‾ ‾‾ ‾‾ ‾‾ .   ‾‾ ‾‾ ‾‾ ‾‾
11 27 14   11 25 15 34 36   44 31 37 34

‾‾ ‾‾ ‾‾ ‾‾ ‾‾   ‾‾ ‾‾ ‾‾   ‾‾ ‾‾ ‾‾ ‾‾ ‾‾
15 27 15 26 44   36 21 15   14 15 41 22 25

‾‾ ‾‾ ‾‾ ‾‾ ‾‾ ‾‾   ‾‾ ‾‾ ‾‾ ‾‾ ‾‾ ‾‾
32 34 31 42 25 35   11 34 31 37 27 14

‾‾ ‾‾ ‾‾ ‾‾   ‾‾   ‾‾ ‾‾ ‾‾ ‾‾ ‾‾ ‾‾ ‾‾
25 22 24 15   11   34 31 11 34 22 27 17

‾‾ ‾‾ ‾‾ ‾‾   ‾‾ ‾‾ ‾‾ ‾‾ ‾‾ ‾‾ ‾‾
25 22 31 27   25 31 31 24 22 27 17

‾‾ ‾‾ ‾‾   ‾‾ ‾‾ ‾‾ ‾‾ ‾‾ ‾‾ ‾‾
16 31 34   35 31 26 15 31 27 15

                                  "
‾‾ ‾‾   ‾‾ ‾‾ ‾‾ ‾‾ ‾‾ ‾‾ .
36 31   14 15 41 31 37 34

1 PETER 5:8

OUR LORD NEVER LEAVES HIS CHILDREN HELPLESS. HE ALWAYS GIVES US A WAY TO STAND AGAINST OUR ENEMY THE DEVIL.
TO FIND OUT HOW, USE THE CODE CHART BELOW TO COMPLETE THE VERSE. USE THE COLUMN GOING DOWN FIRST.

	1	2	3	4	5	6	7
1	A	B	C	D	E	F	G
2	H	I	J	K	L	M	N
3	O	P	Q	R	S	T	U
4	V	W	X	Y	Z		

"

$\overline{35}\ \overline{37}\ \overline{12}\ \overline{26}\ \overline{22}\ \overline{36}\quad \overline{44}\ \overline{31}\ \overline{37}\ \overline{34}\ \overline{}$

$\overline{35}\ \overline{15}\ \overline{25}\ \overline{41}\ \overline{15}\ \overline{35}\ '\ \overline{36}\ \overline{21}\ \overline{15}\ \overline{27}\ '\ \overline{36}\ \overline{31}$

$\overline{17}\ \overline{31}\ \overline{14}\ .\quad \overline{34}\ \overline{15}\ \overline{35}\ \overline{22}\ \overline{35}\ \overline{36}$

$\overline{36}\ \overline{21}\ \overline{15}\quad \overline{14}\ \overline{15}\ \overline{41}\ \overline{22}\ \overline{25}\ ,$

$\overline{11}\ \overline{27}\ \overline{14}\quad \overline{21}\ \overline{15}\quad \overline{42}\ \overline{22}\ \overline{25}\ \overline{25}$

$\overline{16}\ \overline{25}\ \overline{15}\ \overline{15}\quad \overline{16}\ \overline{34}\ \overline{31}\ \overline{26}\quad \overline{44}\ \overline{31}\ \overline{37}\ .\ "$

JAMES 4:7

49

CONNECT-THE-DOTS

"... RESIST THE DEVIL, AND HE WILL FLEE...'

WHAT DO YOU NEED TO DO WHEN THE
DEVIL TEMPTS YOU TO SIN?

AS YOU GO THROUGH THE MAZE, COLLECT
THE LETTERS AND COMPLETE THE
STATEMENT BELOW.

_ _ _ _ _ _ _ THE DEVIL!

WHAT IS THE DEVIL LIKE ?

AS YOU GO THROUGH THE MAZE, COLLECT THE LETTERS AND COMPLETE THE STATEMENT BELOW.

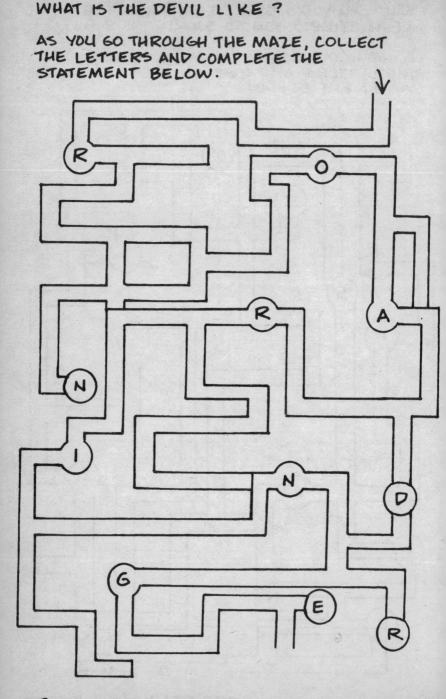

52 THE DEVIL IS LIKE A _ _ _ _ _ _ _ LION!

PSALM 119: 104–105 GIVES ANOTHER DESCRIPTION OF GOD'S WORD, THE BIBLE. USE THE CODE BELOW TO COMPLETE THESE TWO VERSES. USE THE COLUMN GOING DOWN FIRST.

	1	2	3	4	5	6	7
1	A	B	C	D	E	F	G
2	H	I	J	K	L	M	N
3	O	P	Q	R	S	T	U
4	V	W	X	Y	Z		

"

22 17 11 22 27   37 27 14 15 34

35 36 11 27 14 22 27 17   16 34 31 26

44 31 37 34   32 34 15 13 15 32 36 35 ;

36 21 15 34 15 16 31 34 15   22

21 11 36 15   15 41 15 34 44

42 34 31 27 17   32 11 36 21 .

44 31 37 34   42 31 34 14   22 35 11

25 11 26 32   36 31 26 44   16 15 15 36

11 27 14   11   25 22 17 21 36   16 31 34 "

26 44   32 11 36 21 .

53

THE BIBLE IS A LAMP THAT LIGHTS OUR
WAY IN THE DARKNESS OF SIN AND
TEMPTATION.

USING THE GRID, DRAW THE PICTURE
BELOW ON THE NEXT PAGE.

FROM THE PREVIOUS PAGE, USE THE
GRID TO DRAW THE PICTURE FOR YOURSELF.

THE SECOND ENEMY IN OUR WALK WITH THE LORD IS OUR SINFUL NATURE, ALSO KNOWN AS THE "FLESH". THIS SINFUL NATURE OR FLESH IS A PART OF ALL OF US. WE ARE BORN WITH IT.

USE THE CODE CHART BELOW TO MATCH THE CODES WITH LETTERS. USE THE COLUMN GOING DOWN, FIRST, THEN WRITE THE LETTERS IN THE BLANKS.

	1	2	3	4	5	6	7
4			Z	Y	X	W	V
3	O	P	Q	R	S	T	U
2	N	M	L	K	J	I	H
1	A	B	C	D	E	F	G

"
___ ___ ___   ___ ___ ___ ___   ___ ___   ___ ___ ___
36 27 15   11 13 36 35   31 16   36 27 15

___ ___ ___ ___ ___ ___   ___ ___ ___ ___ ___ ___   ___ ___ ___
35 26 21 16 37 23   21 11 36 37 34 15   11 34 15

___ ___ ___ ___ ___ ,   ___ ___ ___ ___ ___ ___ ___ ___ ,
11 21 17 15 34   25 15 11 23 31 37 35 44

___ ___ ___   ___ ___ ___ ___ ___ ___ ___ ,   ___ ___ ___ ___ ___ ___ ,
21 31 36   35 27 11 34 26 21 17   27 11 36 26 21 17

___ ___ ___ ___ ___ ,   ___ ___ ___ ___ ___ ___   ___ ___ ___ ___ ___ ___
23 44 26 21 17   22 11 24 26 21 17   31 36 27 15 34 35

___ ___ ___ ___ ___ ,   ___ ___ ___ ___ ___ ___ ___ ___ ___ ___
11 21 17 34 44   46 31 34 35 27 26 32 26 21 17

___ ___ ___ ___ ___   ___ ___ ___ ___ ,   ___ ___ ___
16 11 23 35 15   17 31 14 35   11 21 14

"
___ ___ ___ ___ ___ ___ ___ ___ ___ ___ .
46 26 36 13 27 13 34 11 16 36

GALATIANS 5:19-21
(CHILDREN'S BIBLE)

56

FIND THE WORDS BELOW IN THE
WORDSEARCH PUZZLE.

WORSHIPING   ANGRY
ACTS   JEALOUSY
SINFUL   HATING
NATURE   LYING
FLESH   SHARING

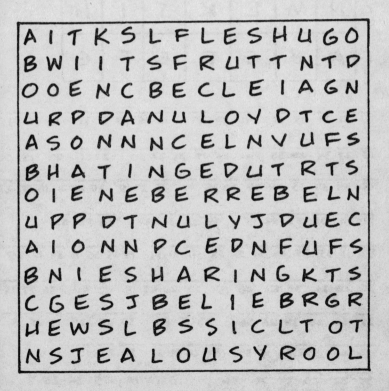

```
A I T K S L F L E S H U G O
B W I I T S F R U T T N T D
O O E N C B E C L E I A G N
U R P D A N U L O Y D T C E
A S O N N N C E L N V U F S
B H A T I N G E D U T R T S
O I E N E B E R R E B E L N
U P P D T N U L Y J D U E C
A I O N N P C E D N F U F S
B N I E S H A R I N G K T S
C G E S J B E L I E B R G R
H E W S L B S S I C L T O T
N S J E A L O U S Y R O O L
```

THE BIBLE TELLS US HOW TO FIGHT THE
DESIRES OF THE SINFUL NATURE.

USE THE CODE CHART BELOW TO MATCH
THE CODES WITH LETTERS. USE THE
COLUMN GOING DOWN, FIRST, THEN WRITE
THE LETTERS IN THE BLANKS.

	1	2	3	4	5	6	7
4			Z	Y	X	W	V
3	O	P	Q	R	S	T	U
2	N	M	L	K	J	I	H
1	A	B	C	D	E	F	G

"

36 27 31 35 15   46 27 31   12 15 23 31 21 17 36 31

13 27 34 26 35 36   25 15 35 37 35   27 11 47 15

13 34 37 13 26 16 26 15 14   36 27 15   35 26 21 16 37 23

21 11 36 37 34 15   46 26 36 27   26 36 35

32 11 35 35 26 31 21 35   11 21 14   14 15 35 26 34 15 35 .

35 26 21 13 15   46 15   23 26 47 15   12 44   36 27 15

35 32 26 34 26 36)   23 15 36   37 35 24 15 15 32

26 21   35 36 15 32   46 26 36 27   36 27 15

35 32 26 34 26 36 . "   GALATIANS 5:24-25

FIND THE WORDS BELOW IN THE WORDSEARCH PUZZLE.

JESUS

SPIRIT

BELONG

PASSIONS

CRUCIFIED

STEP

DESIRES

KEEP

CHRIST

LIVE

```
L F L E S G H U O S F S E F
S F J E S U S T E S F R P T
B E C L E P A R N B E C A E
E U L O V D I D E N U L S Y
L C E L N S U R S N V U S F
O G E D E T R T I D U T I T
N E L D E B E L S T E P O L
G U L Y J D U C C Y J T N E
P C R U C I F I E D S F S F
H A R I N K K T S I N G K T
B E L E I E R G R I E B R G
B S L I V E T H T I C L T O
O U L S Y P C O L S Y R O O
```

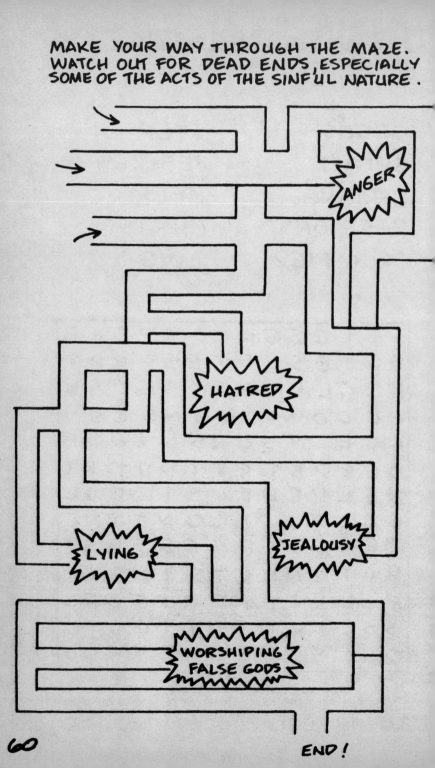

FINISH THE FACE

YOU DO THE DRAWING! DRAW THE
EXPRESSION FOR JOY:

JOY— A FRUIT OF THE HOLY SPIRIT!

FINISH THE FACE

YOU DO THE DRAWING! DRAW THE
EXPRESSION FOR **PEACE**:

PEACE - A FRUIT OF THE HOLY SPIRIT!

FINISH THE FACE

YOU DO THE DRAWING! DRAW THE
EXPRESSION FOR **LOVE**:

LOVE - A FRUIT OF THE HOLY SPIRIT!

FINISH THE FACE

YOU DO THE DRAWING! DRAW THE
EXPRESSION FOR **ANGER**:

ANGER - AN ACT OF THE SINFUL NATURE.

FINISH THE FACE

YOU DO THE DRAWING! DRAW THE
EXPRESSION FOR **HATRED** :

HATRED - AN ACT OF THE SINFUL NATURE.

65

THE THIRD ENEMY IN OUR LIVES WITH GOD
IS THE WORLD.

IT IS NOT THE WORLD IN ITSELF THAT IS
OUR ENEMY AS GOD CREATED THE WORLD.
IT IS SOME OF THE THINGS IN THE WORLD
THAT CAN LEAD US AWAY FROM GOD AND
WHAT HE WANTS US TO DO.

GO THROUGH THE MAZE.

CIRCLE THOSE THINGS THAT COULD BE USED
TO TEMPT YOU TO SIN AND TAKE YOU AWAY
FROM GOD'S PLAN FOR YOUR LIFE.
(YOU MAY BE SURPRISED!)

A LOT OF THINGS CAN
BE USED FOR BAD AS WELL
AS GOOD!

WHAT DOES GOD SAY ABOUT THE THINGS OF THE WORLD?

USE THE CODE CHART BELOW TO MATCH THE CODES WITH LETTERS. USE THE COLUMN GOING DOWN, FIRST, THEN WRITE THE LETTERS IN THE BLANKS.

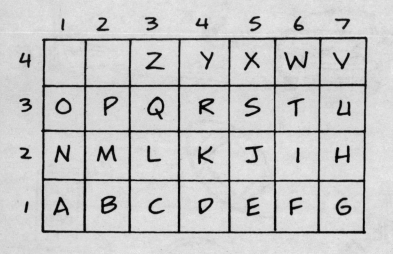

	1	2	3	4	5	6	7
4			Z	Y	X	W	V
3	O	P	Q	R	S	T	U
2	N	M	L	K	J	I	H
1	A	B	C	D	E	F	G

"

‾14‾ ‾31‾ ‾21‾ ‾31‾ ‾36‾ ‾23‾ ‾31‾ ‾47‾ ‾15‾ ‾36‾ ‾27‾ ‾15‾

‾46‾ ‾31‾ ‾34‾ ‾23‾ ‾14‾ ‾31‾ ‾34‾ ‾11‾ ‾21‾ ‾44‾ ‾36‾ ‾27‾ ‾26‾ ‾21‾ ‾1‾

‾26‾ ‾21‾ ‾36‾ ‾27‾ ‾15‾ ‾46‾ ‾31‾ ‾34‾ ‾23‾ ‾14‾ ' ‾26‾ ‾16‾

‾11‾ ‾21‾ ‾44‾ ‾31‾ ‾21‾ ‾15‾ ‾23‾ ‾31‾ ‾47‾ ‾15‾ ‾35‾ ‾36‾ ‾27‾ ‾15‾

‾46‾ ‾31‾ ‾34‾ ‾23‾ ‾14‾ ' ‾36‾ ‾27‾ ‾15‾ ‾23‾ ‾31‾ ‾47‾ ‾15‾ ‾31‾ ‾16‾

‾36‾ ‾27‾ ‾15‾ ‾16‾ ‾11‾ ‾36‾ ‾27‾ ‾15‾ ‾34‾ ‾26‾ ‾35‾ ‾21‾ ‾31‾ ‾36‾

"

‾26‾ ‾21‾ ‾27‾ ‾26‾ ‾22‾ .

1 JOHN 2:15

UNSCRAMBLE THE UNDERLINED WORDS
AND PLACE THEM IN THE CORRECT SPACE
IN THE CROSSWORD GRID ON THE NEXT PAGE.

ACROSS

1. THE HOLY SPIRIT WILL LEAD YOU INTO
   ALL TUHRT .

2. YOUR YBDO IS THE TEMPLE OF THE
   HOLY SPIRIT.

3. YOU HAVE THREE ENEMIES. ONE OF THEM
   IS THE IVDEL .

4. ANOTHER OF YOUR ENEMIES IS YOUR
   FLESH, OR THE SINFUL AERTUN .

DOWN

5. THE HOLY SPIRIT IS ALSO CALLED
   THE LORSECNOU .

6. YOU ARE TO BE CHANGED BY THE
   RENEWING OF YOUR NMDI .

7. THE HOLY SPIRIT WILL PRODUCE
   GOD'S TFIUR IN YOU.

8. YOUR THIRD ENEMY IS THE THINGS
   OF THE RWLDO .

WORD LIST

MIND   DEVIL

BODY   NATURE

COUNSELOR   TRUTH

WORLD   FRUIT

EVEN THOUGH YOU ARE NOW GOD'S CHILD, YOU WILL STILL SIN. WHAT DO YOU DO THEN? TRAVEL THE PATH THAT MAKES A SENTENCE.

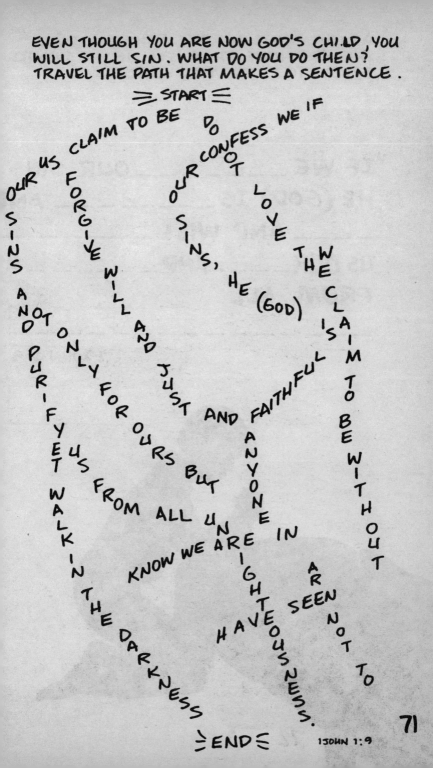

71

1 JOHN 1:9

AFTER GOING THROUGH THE MAZE ON
THE PREVIOUS PAGE, FILL IN THE BLANKS
BELOW TO FINISH THE VERSE.

"IF WE _____ OUR SINS
HE (GOD) IS _____ AND
_____ AND WILL _____
US OUR _____ AND _____ U_
FROM ALL

_____

1 JOHN 1:9

72

FIND THE WORDS BELOW IN THE
WORDSEARCH PUZZLE.

```
U F P D T P C O S P R R T I A
A L O N N F O R G I V E U T H
B L I E W A N T K N L A P D K
C N E S J I F I I W S F U U I
J W S E L T E E N E B E R L E
U S H S N H S P D T N U I O J
S S G E N F S O N N D C F D N
T I W S L U L I E W S G Y T U
E W S G E L N E S J B E L B E
U N R I G H T E O U S N E S S
S L B S N N S H S N I B H A K
S N I B H S S G E N T L E N R
E N T L E H I W S L B P P I T
```

FORGIVE   SINS

FAITHFUL   JUST

PURIFY   CONFESS

UNRIGHTEOUSNESS

OUR LORD JESUS PAID THE PRICE FOR
OUR SINS. HE TOOK OUR PUNISHMENT
BY DYING ON THE CROSS.

USING THE GRID, DRAW THE PICTURE
BELOW ON THE NEXT PAGE.

FROM THE PREVIOUS PAGE, USE THE
GRID TO DRAW THE PICTURE FOR YOURSELF.

ALL CHRISTIANS ARE TEMPTED TO SIN,
TO DO THINGS THAT ARE WRONG. BUT WE
CAN TRUST GOD TO HELP US IN OUR
TIMES OF TEMPTATION.

USE THE CODE CHART BELOW TO MATCH
THE CODES WITH LETTERS. USE THE
COLUMN GOING DOWN, FIRST, THEN WRITE
THE LETTERS IN THE BLANKS.

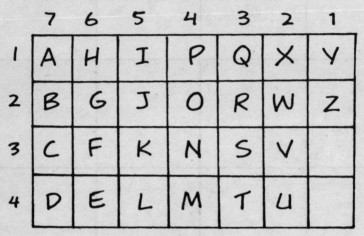

	7	6	5	4	3	2	1
1	A	H	I	P	Q	X	Y
2	B	G	J	O	R	W	Z
3	C	F	K	N	S	V	
4	D	E	L	M	T	U	

"

<u>43</u> <u>16</u> <u>46</u>   <u>24</u> <u>34</u> <u>45</u> <u>11</u>

<u>43</u> <u>46</u> <u>44</u> <u>14</u> <u>43</u> <u>17</u> <u>43</u> <u>15</u> <u>24</u> <u>34</u> <u>33</u>

<u>43</u> <u>16</u> <u>17</u> <u>43</u>   <u>11</u> <u>24</u> <u>42</u>   <u>16</u> <u>17</u> <u>32</u> <u>46</u>

<u>17</u> <u>23</u> <u>46</u>   <u>43</u> <u>16</u> <u>46</u>

<u>43</u> <u>46</u> <u>44</u> <u>14</u> <u>43</u> <u>17</u> <u>43</u> <u>15</u> <u>24</u> <u>34</u> <u>33</u>

<u>43</u> <u>16</u> <u>17</u> <u>43</u> <u>17</u> <u>45</u> <u>45</u> <u>14</u> <u>46</u> <u>24</u> <u>14</u> <u>45</u>

CONT'D NEXT PAGE ..

16 17 32 46 . 27 42 43 11 24 42

37 17 34 43 23 42 33 43 26 24 47 .

16 46 22 15 45 45 34 24 43 45 46 43

11 24 42 27 46 43 46 44 14 43 46 47

44 24 23 46 43 16 17 34 11 24 42

37 17 34 33 43 17 34 47 . 27 42 43

22 16 46 34 11 24 42 17 23 46 9

26 24 47 22 15 45 45 17 45 33 24

26 15 32 46 11 24 42 17 22 17 11

43 24 46 33 37 17 14 46 43 16 17 43

43 46 44 14 43 17 43 15 24 34 .

43 16 46 34 11 24 42 22 15 45 45

27 46 17 27 45 46 43 24

11

33 43 17 34 47 15 43 .

1 CORINTHIANS 10:13
(CHILDREN'S BIBLE)

CONNECT-THE-DOTS

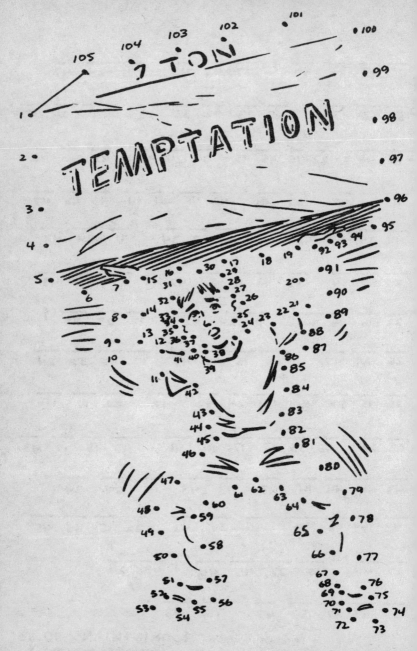

FIGHTING TEMPTATION ON YOUR OWN.

CONNECT-THE-DOTS

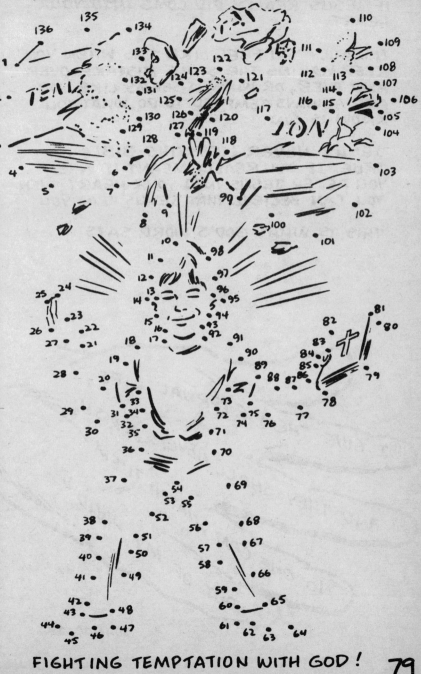

FIGHTING TEMPTATION WITH GOD!

SOMETIMES YOU MAY NOT FEEL LIKE YOU ARE A CHRISTIAN. YOU MAY EVEN WONDER IF JESUS REALLY DID COME INTO YOUR HEART.

USUALLY YOU FEEL LIKE THIS WHEN YOU KEEP MAKING THE SAME MISTAKE OVER AND OVER, OR WHEN IT SEEMS LIKE YOU ARE ALWAYS TEMPTED TO DO WHAT YOU KNOW IS SIN.

JESUS NEVER LIES ; THE BIBLE IS TRUE. IF YOU REALLY MEANT IT WHEN YOU ASKED JESUS INTO YOUR HEART, THEN YOU CAN BELIEVE THAT JESUS IS IN YOU.

THIS IS WHAT GOD'S WORD SAYS :

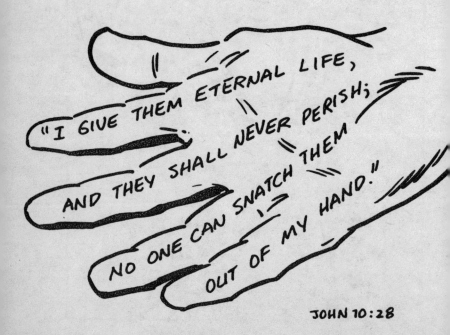

"I GIVE THEM ETERNAL LIFE, AND THEY SHALL NEVER PERISH; NO ONE CAN SNATCH THEM OUT OF MY HAND."

JOHN 10:28

THE ONLY WAY TO HEAVEN IS THROUGH
JESUS CHRIST. HAVING JESUS IN YOUR
HEART MEANS YOU HAVE BEEN GIVEN
ETERNAL LIFE, AND YOU WILL LIVE WITH
GOD FOREVER. THIS IS GOD'S PROMISE
TO YOU!

FIND THE UNDERLINED WORDS IN THE
WORD SEARCH PUZZLE BELOW.

"I <u>GIVE</u> THEM <u>ETERNAL</u>
<u>LIFE</u>, AND THEY <u>SHALL</u> <u>NEVER</u>
<u>PERISH</u>; NO ONE CAN <u>SNATCH</u>
THEM OUT OF MY <u>HAND</u>."

```
S N E S J I F I I W S F U H
J N P E T E R N A L B R E L
U S A S N H S E D T N U I O
P Q G T N F T V N N D C F D
T S W S C U L E E W S G H T
I H H B A H E R T L E N A C
T A E H I W S L B E P I N E
L L E P N E G E F L E T D C
N L S E D T N I I O J N F O
E F S O N M L C V D N W A N
T U L E D W G S V E U J I F
E L N E B J B L S B E L T E
G P E R I S H N E S S N U S
```

FROM THE START OF YOUR CHRISTIAN LIFE TO THE END OF IT, YOU WILL ALWAYS STAY IN THE HAND OF THE LORD JESUS.

LIFE WILL NOT ALWAYS BE EASY, BUT JESUS WILL GET YOU THROUGH!

FIND YOUR WAY THROUGH THE MAZE OF LIFE.

START

END

HOW TO DRAW THE HAND

STEP 1.

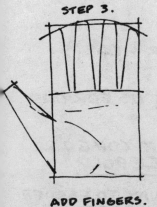

DRAW A RECTANGLE.

STEP 2.

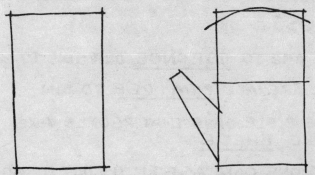

ADD A CONE SHAPE FOR THE THUMB, A LINE ACROSS THE MIDDLE, AND A CURVE ACROSS THE TOP.

STEP 3.

ADD FINGERS.

STEP 4.

FINISH BY ADDING DETAILS.

TRY IT FOR YOURSELF. YOU HAVE ROOM BELOW FOR TWO PICTURES. USE YOUR OWN HAND AS A GUIDE.

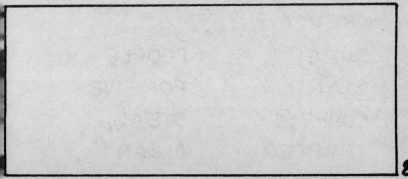

UNSCRAMBLE THE UNDERLINED WORDS
AND PLACE THEM IN THE CROSSWORD GRID
ON THE NEXT PAGE.

ACROSS

1. WE ARE TO SSFCNOE OUR SINS TO GOD.

2. WE ARE ALL PTMTDEE TO SIN.

3. THE BIBLE SAYS THAT PEOPLE ARE
   LIKE PHESE.

4. NO ONE CAN ASETL US OUT OF GOD'S
   HAND.

DOWN

1. GOD WILL MAKE OUR HEARTS
   CLNAE AND NEW.

2. GOD WILL EFGRVOI US FOR OUR
   SINS.

3. THE TEMPTATIONS THAT COME ARE
   WHAT COME TO ALL EEPOLP.

4. GOD WILL GIVE US A WAY TO ESCAPE
   TEMPTATION SO WE CAN ASDNT.

WORD LIST

SHEEP	PEOPLE
STAND	FORGIVE
CONFESS	STEAL
TEMPTED	CLEAN

84

IF YOU REMEMBER, WHEN YOU INVITE
JESUS CHRIST INTO YOUR LIFE, YOUR BODY
BECOMES THE TEMPLE OF GOD'S HOLY SPIRIT

IN OTHER WORDS, YOUR BODY BECOMES THE
"HOUSE" THAT THE HOLY SPIRIT DWELLS IN.
AS YOU LIVE IN A HOUSE THAT NEEDS
CLEANING, SO DOES YOUR "BODY-HOUSE"
NEED CLEANING. THE HOLY SPIRIT WANTS
TO CLEAN UP WRONG THINKING AND
ACTIONS.

THE HOUSE WITHOUT JESUS:

COLOR THE PICTURE.

NOW THAT THE HOLY SPIRIT LIVES IN YOU,
HE IS GOING TO WANT TO CLEAN AND EVEN
CHANGE SOME THINGS IN HIS HOUSE!

THIS TAKES TIME BUT THE RESULT IS THAT
YOU ARE MADE FREE AND MUCH HAPPIER.
AND JUST LIKE A NICE CLEAN HOUSE,
YOU ARE MORE INVITING TO OTHERS.
PEOPLE WILL WANT TO BE AROUND YOU,
AND YOU CAN SHARE WITH THEM WHAT
JESUS HAS DONE IN YOUR LIFE!

THE HOUSE WITH JESUS:

COLOR THE PICTURE.   87

GO THROUGH THE HOUSE BELOW AND PICK UP THOSE THINGS THAT GOD WOULD CLEAN OUT. WRITE THEM IN THE BLANK SPACES BELOW.

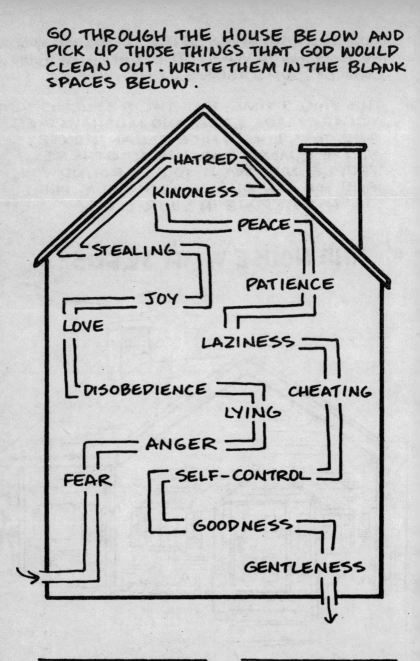

AGAIN, IT IS THE WORK OF THE HOLY SPIRIT
THAT DOES THE CLEANING IN US. HE ONLY
NEEDS US TO BE WILLING TO LET HIM DO
THAT WORK.

GOD'S WORD GIVES US A PROMISE!

FIND THE UNDERLINED WORDS IN THE
WORDSEARCH PUZZLE BELOW.

"BE <u>CONFIDENT</u> OF THIS, THAT
HE WHO <u>BEGAN</u> A <u>GOOD</u> <u>WORK</u>
IN YOU WILL <u>CARRY</u> IT ON TO
THE <u>FINISH</u> UNTIL <u>JESUS</u>
<u>CHRIST</u> COMES AGAIN."

PHILIPPIANS 1:6
(CHILDREN'S BIBLE)

```
P Q G T N F B V N N D C Y D
T S W S C U L E E W S R H T
I W O R K H E R G L R N A C
F A E H I W S L B A P I N C
I L E P N E G L C E N I N H
N Q G T G F T V N N A W C R
I U L C O N F I D E N T P I
S L N H O J B L S B G H F S
H P E R D S H J E S U S W T
E L N E B J B X Y B Z T L D
```

PICTURE YOURSELF AS A SOLDIER!
YOU ARE NOW A SOLDIER FOR JESUS
CHRIST, AND HE GIVES US EVERYTHING
WE NEED TO WIN THE BATTLE.

USE THE CODE CHART BELOW TO MATCH
THE CODES WITH LETTERS. USE THE
COLUMN GOING DOWN FIRST, THEN WRITE
THE LETTERS IN THE BLANKS.

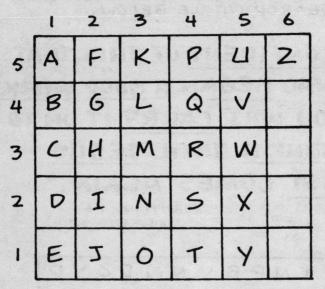

	1	2	3	4	5	6
5	A	F	K	P	U	Z
4	B	G	L	Q	V	
3	C	H	M	R	W	
2	D	I	N	S	X	
1	E	J	O	T	Y	

$\overline{52}$ $\overline{22}$ $\overline{23}$ $\overline{51}$ $\overline{43}$ $\overline{43}$ $\overline{15}$, $\overline{41}$ $\overline{11}$

$\overline{24}$ $\overline{14}$ $\overline{34}$ $\overline{13}$ $\overline{23}$ $\overline{42}$ $\overline{22}$ $\overline{23}$ $\overline{14}$ $\overline{32}$ $\overline{1}$

$\overline{43}$ $\overline{13}$ $\overline{34}$ $\overline{21}$ $\overline{51}$ $\overline{23}$ $\overline{21}$ $\overline{22}$ $\overline{23}$ $\overline{32}$ $\overline{22}$ $\overline{2}$

$\overline{33}$ $\overline{22}$ $\overline{42}$ $\overline{32}$ $\overline{14}$ $\overline{15}$ $\overline{54}$ $\overline{13}$ $\overline{35}$ $\overline{11}$ $\overline{34}$

CONT'D NEXT PAGE..

$\overline{54}\ \overline{55}\ \overline{14}\quad \overline{13}\ \overline{23}\quad \overline{14}\ \overline{32}\ \overline{11}\quad \overline{52}\ \overline{55}\ \overline{43}\ \overline{43}$

$\overline{51}\ \overline{34}\ \overline{33}\ \overline{13}\ \overline{34}\quad \overline{13}\ \overline{52}\quad \overline{42}\ \overline{13}\ \overline{21}$

$\overline{24}\ \overline{13}\quad \overline{14}\ \overline{32}\ \overline{51}\ \overline{14}\quad \overline{15}\ \overline{13}\ \overline{55}\quad \overline{31}\ \overline{51}\ \overline{23}$

$\overline{14}\ \overline{51}\ \overline{53}\ \overline{11}\quad \overline{15}\ \overline{13}\ \overline{55}\ \overline{34}\quad \overline{24}\ \overline{14}\ \overline{51}\ \overline{23}\ \overline{21}$

$\overline{51}\ \overline{42}\ \overline{51}\ \overline{22}\ \overline{24}\ \overline{23}\ \overline{14}\ ,\quad \overline{14}\ \overline{32}\ \overline{11}$

$\overline{21}\ \overline{11}\ \overline{45}\ \overline{22}\ \overline{43}\ \overline{24}\quad \overline{24}\ \overline{31}\ \overline{32}\ \overline{11}\ \overline{33}\ \overline{11}\ \overline{24}\ ."$

EPHESIANS 6:10-11

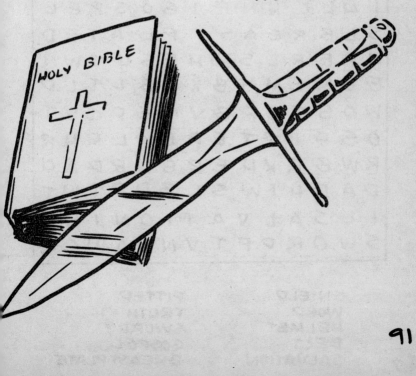

FIND THE UNDERLINED WORDS IN THE
WORDSEARCH PUZZLE BELOW.

" STAND FIRM THEN, WITH THE BELT OF
TRUTH BUCKLED AROUND YOUR WAIST,
WITH THE BREAST PLATE OF RIGHTEOUSNESS
IN PLACE , AND WITH YOUR FEET FITTED WITH
THE READINESS THAT COMES FROM THE
GOSPEL OF PEACE . IN ADDITION TO ALL
THIS, TAKE UP THE SHIELD OF FAITH, WITH
WHICH YOU CAN EXTINGUISH ALL THE
FLAMING ARROWS OF THE EVIL ONE. TAKE
THE HELMET OF SALVATION AND THE
SWORD OF THE SPIRIT, WHICH IS THE
WORD OF GOD. "

EPHESIANS 6: 14-17

THIS IS THE FULL ARMOR OF GOD!

```
I U L C H N F I G O S P E L
S L B R E A S T P L A T E D
H P E R L S H H E S U T W N
E L N E M J B X I B L T L D
W Q G T E F B V N E D C Y T
O S F I T T E D B W L R H R
R W B R K H E R G L R D A U
D A E H I W S L B D P T W T
I L S A L V A T I O N I N H
S W O R D F T V N N A W C R
```

SHIELD	FITTED
WORD	TRUTH
HELMET	SWORD
BELT	GOSPEL
SALVATION	BREASTPLATE

FILL IN THE BLANKS.

_ W _ _ D _ R _ _ E
_ _ P _ R _

_ E _ _ E _ O _
S _ _ V _ _ I _ _

S _ _ E _ _ F
_ H _ O _ _ L

B _ _ _ O _ R T _

_ _ E S _ _ A _ _
R _ _ H _ O _ N _ _ S

_ _ I E _ _ _ F
F _ _ T _

THE FULL ARMOR OF GOD!   93

FINISH THE PICTURE.

DRAW OVER THE DOTTED LINES TO "DRESS" IN THE ARMOR OF GOD.

FIND YOUR WAY THROUGH THE BATTLEFIELD OF LIFE. WATCH OUT FOR TEMPTATION AND SIN!

END

95

DO YOU REMEMBER OUR THREE ENEMIES,
THE *WORLD*, THE *FLESH* (OR SINFUL NATURE),
AND THE *DEVIL*?

WE CALL THE BATTLE AGAINST THESE
ENEMIES *SPIRITUAL WARFARE*!

GOD'S WORD HAS SOMETHING TO SAY
ABOUT THIS WARFARE.

" FOR OUR STRUGGLE (OUR BATTLE) IS
NOT AGAINST FLESH AND BLOOD, BUT
AGAINST THE RULERS, AGAINST THE
AUTHORITIES, AGAINST THE POWERS OF
THIS DARK WORLD AND AGAINST THE
SPIRITUAL FORCES OF EVIL IN THE
HEAVENLY REALMS (THE UNSEEN
SPIRITUAL WORLD AROUND US)."

EPHESIANS 6:12

FIND THE WORDS BELOW IN THE
WORDSEARCH .

```
      C H B F L G O
    L B R E F L E S H
     E B R L I H O E S U
  S E L N T V J B X O B
    T Q G E W F B V W D C Y
  D P R F L T O S D P X D
    R A U T H O R I T I E S
  W D N H G V W S L B D P T W
    P L S A G V D T D N Z H
  H E A V E N L Y V G J Q C R
    L N R U L E R S W L
      B R K H S N G L R
      H W   L
```

FLESH   RULERS

EVIL   BLOOD

WORLD   HEAVENLY

STRUGGLE   AUTHORITIES

NOW IT IS TIME TO START LIVING YOUR LIFE AS A CHILD OF GOD.

THERE ARE MANY THINGS IN LIFE THAT CAN DISTRACT US, OR LEAD US AWAY, FROM JESUS.

WHAT DOES JESUS SAY WE SHOULD DO?

UNSCRAMBLE THE WORDS AND PUT THEM IN THE RIGHT PLACES IN THE VERSE BELOW.

" LET US _XFI_ OUR EYES ON _SEUJS_, THE _RATUHO_ AND PERFECTER OF OUR _AFHIT_, WHO FOR THE _OYJ_ SET _EBRFEO_ HIM ENDURED THE _ORSCS_, SCORNING ITS _MHSEA_, AND SAT _WODN_ AT THE RIGHT _NDHA_ OF THE _HTNROE_ OF GOD."

HEBREWS 12:2

" LET US ____ OUR EYES ON _____, THE _____ AND PERFECTER OF OUR _____, WHO FOR THE ___ SET _____ HIM ENDURED THE _____, SCORNING ITS _____, AND SAT _____ AT THE RIGHT _____ OF THE _____ OF GOD."

WORDSEARCH

```
I D L J G Q P A N G E L
G J A I L I U T K P W U
A O N X H D S L A V E C
D H D S A O G E B O T R
H Z R Z D L R T I R X F
P O M N G S C T A B Q V
W T Y J U D G E M E N T
M C S J O E H R Y I F K
W O H L B Y A S T O R M
V I S I O N E F J S E V
```

JUDGEMENT

JOY

HEART

LETTERS

JAIL

WORSHIP

IDOLS

VISION

SLAVE

ANGEL

STORM

GOD

WORDSEARCH

```
B T W I E L D E R S D A J
I G J A H T N I Y N H O C
V E E T H I O P I A N Z P
H N R V P C Z F U P Y I B
G T U S H M B X G S L X Q
O I S T G R J Q S I W D C
Q L A L S T E P H E N B F
N E L D O C W P A J E M G
D P E A N T I O C H A K D
K U M E Z F S T O N I N G
J V D L U T H E L R Y K R
E M F K F I W S X N H J E
```

SEEK	ELDERS
STEPHEN	STONING
PHILIP	ANTIOCH
ETHIOPIAN	DEATH
JEWISH	GENTILE
JERUSALEM	FIND

WORDSEARCH

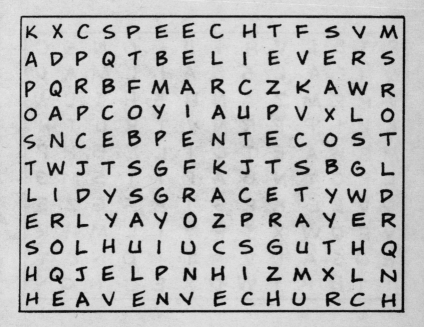

```
K X C S P E E C H T F S V M
A D P Q T B E L I E V E R S
P Q R B F M A R C Z K A W R
O A P C O Y I A U P V X L O
S N C E B P E N T E C O S T
T W J T S G F K J T S B G L
L I D Y S G R A C E T Y W D
E R L Y A Y O Z P R A Y E R
S O L H U I U C S G U T H Q
H Q J E L P N H I Z M X L N
H E A V E N V E C H U R C H
```

HOLY SPIRIT   BELIEVERS
HEAVEN   APOSTLE
PENTECOST   GRACE
PETER   SPEECH
ACTS   CHURCH
PRAYER   SAUL

WORDSEARCH

```
R T B L V H I U L O N S O
Q H E A L S B A I L M A D
V P F M Z A N H S H J L W
C K I T P R N Y T R U T H
M G L A E T C I L Y B H P
L P O T N B A P T I S M G
O D E G K F S T A F G Z E
V F Q W X J F Y I L M H K
E Q S A L V A T I O N C T
I T E R T W D X E J N Q V
```

SALVATION   FAITH

BAPTISM   LIFE

WAY   TEMPTATION

HEALS   ETERNAL

TRUTH   SALT

LIGHT   LOVE

WORDSEARCH

```
H W F A T H E R T E O
E Y K L R K V B S O C
M J X I U S C L X M F
L A S L A U E W N Y D
R M T K V P J G L D J
H E S T S U A O Y B E
B S G O H J H D H P S
F Z G C N E T Z I N U
Q M A R K P W M A J S
G D T R I N I T Y Q N
```

HOLY	JOHN
SON	GOSPELS
LUKE	FATHER
MATTHEW	MARK
JAMES	TRINITY
GOD	JESUS

SEARCH FOR IT
FIND THE NAMES OF THE FOUR GOSPELS BELOW.

(HINT: THE FIRST FOUR BOOKS OF THE NEW
TESTAMENT ARE CALLED THE GOSPELS.)

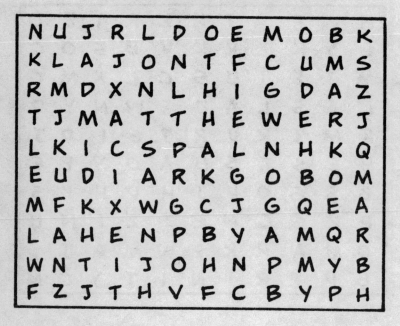

```
N U J R L D O E M O B K
K L A J O N T F C U M S
R M D X N L H I G D A Z
T J M A T T H E W E R J
L K I C S P A L N H K Q
E U D I A R K G O B O M
M F K X W G C J G Q E A
L A H E N P B Y A M Q R
W N T I J O H N P M Y B
F Z J T H V F C B Y P H
```

_____   _____

_____   _____

WORDSEARCH

```
B U E S T H E R T P H R Y
Q E A M R E Z E K I E L C
T P S A L M S G J Z D L H
S M L N E H E M I A H S R
F O D O Z C F L S Y B C O
I G L A R H E J I R M X N
J P X O A U A V E S O I I
S K N I M R B V W K H Q C
B N A F N O O B D Q K A L
O S I H J R N H G B V L E
I T C E P W Z P K I N G S
```

NEHEMIAH   ESTHER
ELISHA   EZRA
JOB   ISAIAH
SOLOMON   PROVERBS
PSALMS   CHRONICLES
KINGS   EZEKIEL

WORDSEARCH

```
B I M Y H Q L X T R I A L S F
G F A I T H V D N R O M O J P
R C O S G P F Q C W U C R U C
S A W A B C S H A L D T D E E
H E A R T I D A V I D N H O C
E W S E R P J K L X B V E G A
P R A I S E P I V M P G U Z I
H E Z R N J E B A E U F Q S G
E R Q E L N I T M F G T D O H
R V D U R D E N E S Y N K N B
D S J P F H Z R K X M O T G T
```

HEART   REFUGE
TRUTH   TRIALS
SINNER   SONG
PSALM   PRAISE
SHEPHERD   LORD
DAVID   FAITH

WORDSEARCH

```
L O M J S A M U E L U E
A E X O D U S B Y O S R
N W V F S R A L T Z J G
U J G I I E O D N L T E
M U R U T H S K D Q P N
B D E H Y I B S U M I E
E G P X S M C A V C W S
R E C J O S H U A F V I
S S A G Q L N L S H K S
```

SAUL	EXODUS
GENESIS	JOSHUA
LEVITICUS	SAMUEL
RUTH	NUMBERS
JUDGES	MOSES

WORDSEARCH

```
K I N G X J N C L J Q R
A C H I J O R D A N O S
P R O M I S E J I K D H
M U T P N H B S G N O E
V D R I A U B V A A C B
C O V E N A N T R R F R
H L A W S E S A A M Q E
B U S H W T H F Y G K W
T D F Z E P B O E P L S
```

JOSHUA   KING
JORDAN   LAWS
SIN   REST
COVENANT   HEBREWS
PROMISE   BUSH
STANDS   PHARAOH

GOD'S PROMISE

GOD HAS GIVEN ABRAM A NEW NAME THAT MEANS
FATHER OF NATIONS. HE HAS PROMISED ABRAM A SON.

CROSS OUT EVERY LETTER THAT APPEARS FOUR TIMES—
WRITE THE REMAING LETTERS IN ORDER TO FIND HIS NEW NAME.

```
C P A D L W E S I
F Y T G I B Q G Q
W E S K Q F Q C Y
R L Y P A W Y K G
K T H C D T S D I
S F K P E T A W G
C L D M E L P F I
```

WHAT IS HIS NEW NAME ? _____

WORDSEARCH

```
I D S P C G A K M V U O D K S N H
O H O L Y S P I R I T D P I E K P
U D Y W O C W M X Z X B T D R J M
G T R F N X E O I J B E R W P N J
Q R B I H Y A L R T Q A B A E H S
T E L O Z A B P F D G J Z Q N P F
N E D E N G P Y K F L H N I T O D
J Q E X A W V N J U A K W L R J W
G L Y S H Q K T E M P T E D S I C
F D E V A R Z Y C W L H B C T G H
A S X K W N Q O D U N G M O B T Q
B D S E R V G M Z R V D B T R I W
S R A C J C U E Z A Q T R A U M L
E D T M N X V P L F A G E F Y L V
M T D C R E A T I O N H X S V U G
L R Y E O Z U F M Y C H K F T N I
```

ADAM   ANGEL
CREATION   HOLY SPIRIT
SWORD   EARTH
TREE   EVE
SERPENT   TEMPTED
 GARDEN   EDEN

110

WORDSEARCH

```
I X L O B N Z U N F J A Z T U Y F
E B M Z A D O K K I M H L O R D A
P O R H B P F V X G L K Y D I G L
Y L T O A K N A W O H T Y C A N S
R A C W D B H U T C G B F M H D M
N S E M O E A X U H J W I S D O M
V F O C Q B A T T L E A P Q L Z G
C J K L X D Z B H J V R V A K N R
I H W O O R B G Q S O M S W I R I
T K D Y U M S E A W H B A K F Q E
D E G A J C O L F I A E I G L M F
S Q V L P T S N Z K P N B N Y U H
J P M A R R I E S H T X E A S R I
```

BATHSHEBA	ABSALOM
URIAH	FATHER
MARRIES	LOYAL
LORD	BATTLE
NATHAN	KING
GRIEF	ZADOK
SOLOMON	WISDOM

WORDSEARCH

```
C I P L H O S P T S A G
Q A F A T Z F D E R W H
K E D R L G P N M I R V
Q U B M J A R G P J N I
J H S K E Y C K L X J M
E T W G M B W E E P O H
R D L R P N S A F Z N U
U C A X W U A N K Q A J
S Q A N O I N T E D T B
A D H H G Y U M H I H Y
L N E B C E L W O A A O
E T L T O A R K D P N U
M V J E V Y D X F M C Z
```

WEEP	JERUSALEM
DANGER	PALACE
ARMY	ARK
JONATHAN	TEMPLE
ANOINTED	NATHAN
JUDAH	HOUSE

FIND THE WORDS

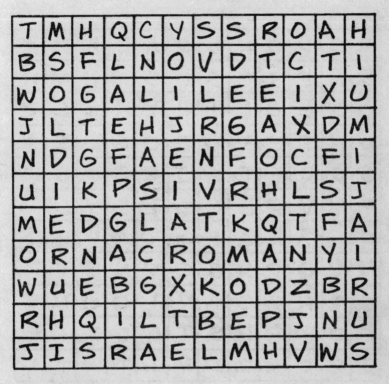

T	M	H	Q	C	Y	S	S	R	O	A	H
B	S	F	L	N	O	V	D	T	C	T	I
W	O	G	A	L	I	L	E	E	I	X	U
J	L	T	E	H	J	R	G	A	X	D	M
N	D	G	F	A	E	N	F	O	C	F	I
U	I	K	P	S	I	V	R	H	L	S	J
M	E	D	G	L	A	T	K	Q	T	F	A
O	R	N	A	C	R	O	M	A	N	Y	I
W	U	E	B	G	X	K	O	D	Z	B	R
R	H	Q	I	L	T	B	E	P	J	N	U
J	I	S	R	A	E	L	M	H	V	W	S

ROMAN   JAIRUS
FAITH   HEALING
GALILEE   SOLDIER
BOAT   ISRAEL

FIND THE WORDS

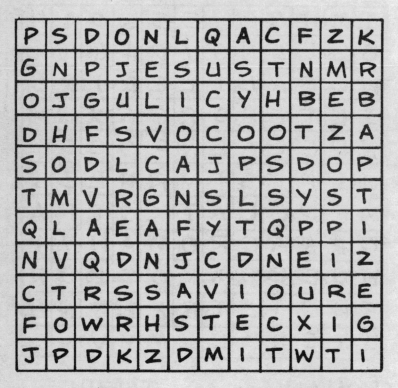

P	S	D	O	N	L	Q	A	C	F	Z	K
G	N	P	J	E	S	U	S	T	N	M	R
O	J	G	U	L	I	C	Y	H	B	E	B
D	H	F	S	V	O	C	O	O	T	Z	A
S	O	D	L	C	A	J	P	S	D	O	P
T	M	V	R	G	N	S	L	S	Y	S	T
Q	L	A	E	A	F	Y	T	Q	P	P	I
N	V	Q	D	N	J	C	D	N	E	I	Z
C	T	R	S	S	A	V	I	O	U	R	E
F	O	W	R	H	S	T	E	C	X	I	G
J	P	D	K	Z	D	M	I	T	W	T	I

JESUS   BAPTIZE

SPIRIT   GOD

JOHN   SAVIOUR

JORDAN   DOVE

FIND THE WORDS

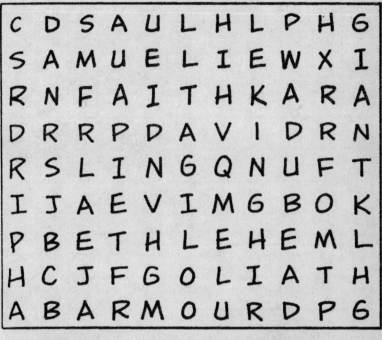

```
C D S A U L H L P H G
S A M U E L I E W X I
R N F A I T H K A R A
D R R P D A V I D R N
R S L I N G Q N U F T
I J A E V I M G B O K
P B E T H L E H E M L
H C J F G O L I A T H
A B A R M O U R D P G
```

SAUL
ISRAEL
KING
SAMUEL
BETHLEHEM
DAVID

HEART
GOLIATH
GIANT
ARMOUR
SLING
FAITH

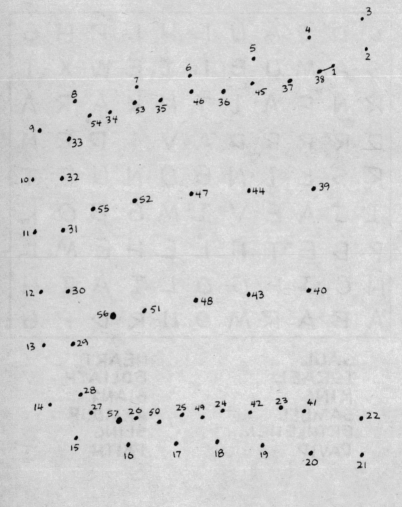

CONNECT THE DOTS

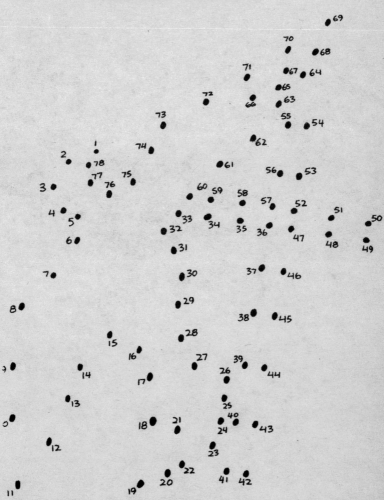

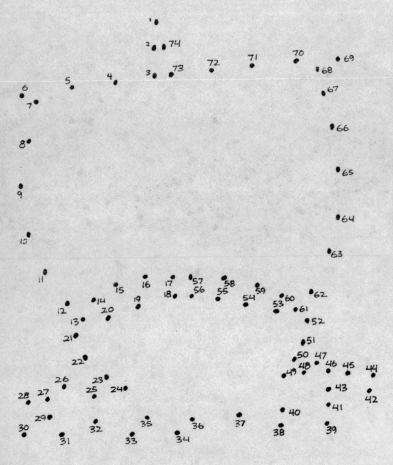

CONNECT THE DOTS

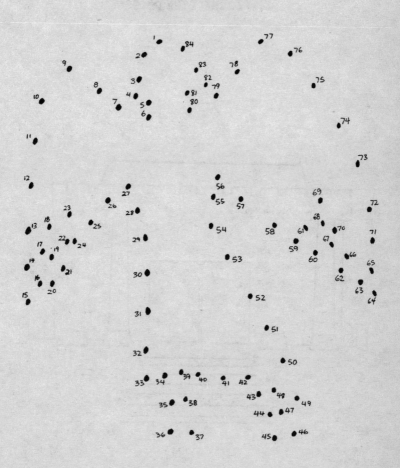

HELP BUILD THE TEMPLE
CONNECT THE DOTS

CONNECT THE DOTS
YOUNG DAVID WENT TO BATTLE AGAINST--?

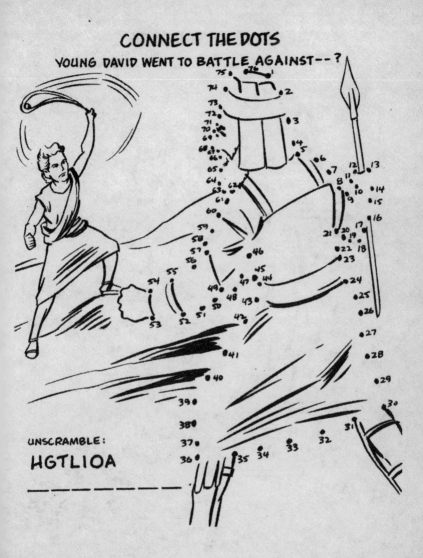

UNSCRAMBLE:

HGTLIOA

——— ——— ——— ——— ——— ——— ———

CONNECT THE DOTS

JESUS, THE _____ OF JUDAH!

CONNECT THE DOTS
PETER WALKS ON THE WATER

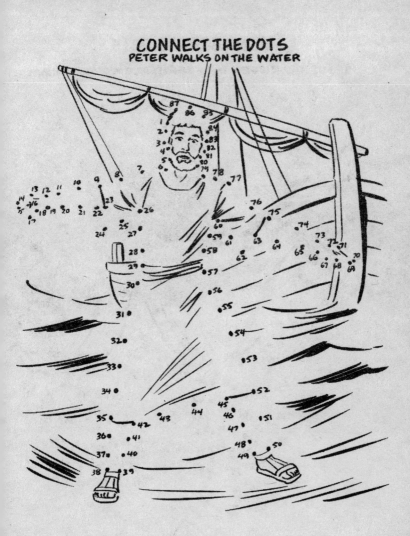

CONNECT THE DOTS

JESUS HAD RIDDEN INTO JERUSALEM ON THIS ANIMAL

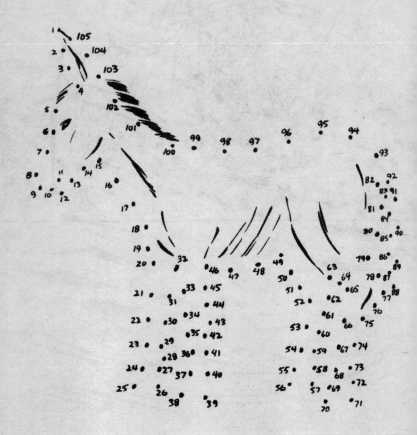

CONNECT THE DOTS

SAUL MET JESUS ON THE ROAD TO DAMASCUS.

GOD CREATED A BEAUTIFUL GARDEN FOR ADAM AND EVE TO LIVE IN. THE SERPENT TEMPTED THEM TO DISOBEY GOD. WHICH TREE DID THEY EAT FROM WHEN THEY SINNED?

BANANA TREE

HOT DOG TREE

CHOCOLATE TREE

ICE CREAM TREE

THE TREE OF THE KNOWLEDGE OF GOOD AND EVIL

COLOR THE TREE - AND ADAM AND EVE TOO!

ANSWER: THE TREE OF THE KNOWLEDGE OF GOOD AND EVIL.

SOLVE THE PUZZLE AND COLOR THE PICTURE

GOD GAVE A PROMISE TO NEVER DESTROY THE WORLD AGAIN
BY WATER. WHAT SIGN DID HE GIVE OF HIS PROMISE?
USE THE CIRCLED LETTERS TO FIND THE ANSWERS.

NOAH BUILT AN __ O __ .

__ __ O __ WAS THE ONLY GOOD MAN LEFT.

IT WOULD __ __ O __ FOR FORTY DAYS AND NIGHTS.

THE __ O __ __ __ __ __ CAME IN TWO BY TWO.

THE O __ __ IS THE FRONT OF THE BOAT.

GOD __ __ O __ __ __ __ __ TO SAVE NOAH.

NOAH OPENED A __ __ __ __ __ O TO SEND

OUT A DOVE.

ANSWERS: ARK, NOAH, RAIN, ANIMALS, BOW, PROMISED, WINDOW
=RAINBOW

127

THE TOWER OF BABEL

PEOPLE BUILT A HIGH TOWER TO PROVE HOW POWERFUL AND SMART THEY WERE — BUT GOD WAS NOT PLEASED.

UNSCRAMBLE THE WORDS AND PUT THEM IN PROPER ORDER TO FIND OUT WHAT GOD DID TO STOP THEM.

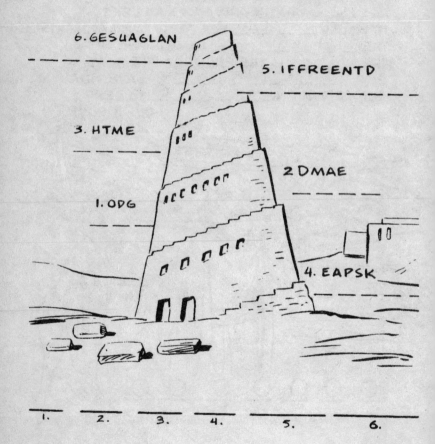

6. GESUAGLAN

5. IFFREENTD

3. HTME

2. DMAE

1. ODG

4. EAPSK

1. _____ 2. _____ 3. _____ 4. _____ 5. _____ 6. _____

WHATEVER HAPPENED TO JOSEPH?
USING THE CODE BELOW, FIND THE ANSWER.

A	B	C	D	E	F	G	H	I	J	K	L	M
26	25	24	23	22	21	20	19	18	17	16	15	14

N	O	P	Q	R	S	T	U	V	W	X	Y	Z
13	12	11	10	9	8	7	6	5	4	3	2	1

17 12 8 22 11 19   4 26 8 25 15 22 8 8 22 23

25 2   20 12 23   26 13 23   14 26 23 22   26

9 6 15 22 9   18 13 22 20 2 11 7 .

ANSWER: JOSEPH IS BLESSED BY GOD AND MADE A RULER IN EGYPT.

UNSCRAMBLE THE LETTERS BELOW TO FIND THE NAME OF:

THE SEVENTH BOOK OF THE BIBLE:

SJEUGD

___ ___ ___ ___ ___ ___

THE EIGHTH BOOK OF THE BIBLE:

HRTU

___ ___ ___ ___

THE NINTH BOOK OF THE BIBLE:

LSEA1UM

___ ___ ___ ___ ___ ___ ___

THE TENTH BOOK OF THE BIBLE:

LM2USAE

___ ___ ___ ___ ___ ___ ___

ANSWERS: JUDGES, RUTH, 1 SAMUEL, 2 SAMUEL

LOOK IN YOUR BIBLE

GOD REVEALED HIS NAME TO MOSES.
WHAT WAS GOD'S NAME ?

LOOK UP EXODUS 3 : 13 - 14.

ANSWER:_____

ANSWER: "I AM WHO I AM."

131

USE THE CODE BELOW TO ANSWER THE QUESTIONS.

A	B	C	D	E	F	G	H	I	J	K	L	M
26	25	24	23	22	21	20	19	18	17	16	15	14

N	O	P	Q	R	S	T	U	V	W	X	Y	Z
13	12	11	10	9	8	7	6	5	4	3	2	1

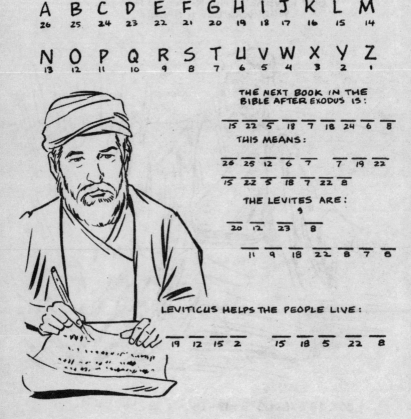

THE NEXT BOOK IN THE
BIBLE AFTER EXODUS IS:

___ ___ ___ ___ ___ ___ ___ ___ ___
15 22 5 18 7 18 24 6 8

THIS MEANS:

___ ___ ___ ___ ___   ___ ___ ___
26 25 12 6 7   7 19 22

___ ___ ___ ___ ___ ___ ___
15 22 5 18 7 22 8

THE LEVITES ARE:

___ ___ ___ ___
20 12 23 8

___ ___ ___ ___ ___ ___ ___
11 9 18 22 8 7 8

LEVITICUS HELPS THE PEOPLE LIVE:

___ ___ ___ ___   ___ ___ ___ ___ ___
19 12 15 2   15 18 5 22 8

UNSCRAMBLE THE LETTERS BELOW TO NAME
THIS BOOK OF THE BIBLE

(IT'S A HARD ONE, SO YOU GET A LITTLE HELP ON THIS.)

Y D M E O U N T O E R

_ E _ _ E _ O _ O _ _

HOW MANY YEARS WERE THE ISRAELITES
IN THE DESERT?

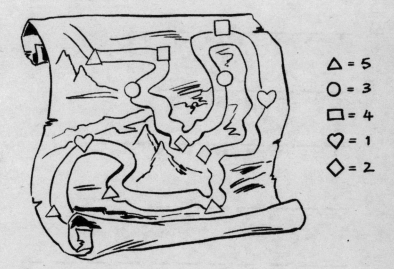

△ = 5

○ = 3

▢ = 4

♡ = 1

◇ = 2

△ + ▢ + ○ + ◇ + ○ + ▢ + ♡ + ◇ + △ + △ + ♡ + △ = ____

ANSWER: ____ YEARS

USE THE CODE BELOW TO NAME THE FIRST FIVE BOOKS
OF THE BIBLE.

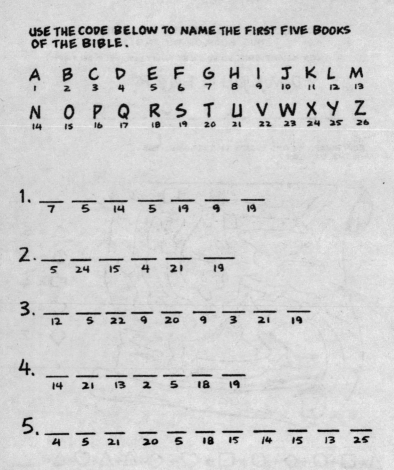

A B C D E F G H I J K L M
1 2 3 4 5 6 7 8 9 10 11 12 13

N O P Q R S T U V W X Y Z
14 15 16 17 18 19 20 21 22 23 24 25 26

1. $\overline{}$ $\overline{}$ $\overline{}$ $\overline{}$ $\overline{}$ $\overline{}$ $\overline{}$
     7   5 14   5 19 9 19

2. $\overline{}$ $\overline{}$ $\overline{}$ $\overline{}$ $\overline{}$ $\overline{}$
     5 24 15 4 21 19

3. $\overline{}$ $\overline{}$ $\overline{}$ $\overline{}$ $\overline{}$ $\overline{}$ $\overline{}$ $\overline{}$ $\overline{}$
    12 5 22 9 20 9 3 21 19

4. $\overline{}$ $\overline{}$ $\overline{}$ $\overline{}$ $\overline{}$ $\overline{}$ $\overline{}$
    14 21 13 2 5 18 19

5. $\overline{}$ $\overline{}$ $\overline{}$ $\overline{}$ $\overline{}$ $\overline{}$ $\overline{}$ $\overline{}$ $\overline{}$ $\overline{}$ $\overline{}$
     4 5 21 20 5 18 15 14 15 13 25

134

USE THE CODE BELOW TO ANSWER THE QUESTIONS.

A	B	C	D	E	F	G	H	I	J	K	L	M
26	25	24	23	22	21	20	19	18	17	16	15	14

N	O	P	Q	R	S	T	U	V	W	X	Y	Z
13	12	11	10	9	8	7	6	5	4	3	2	1

WHO SHOWED HIMSELF TO MOSES IN THE BURNING BUSH?

$\overline{7}$ $\overline{19}$ $\overline{22}$ $\overline{26}$ $\overline{13}$ $\overline{20}$ $\overline{22}$ $\overline{15}$ $\overline{12}$ $\overline{21}$ $\overline{7}$ $\overline{19}$ $\overline{22}$ $\overline{15}$ $\overline{12}$ $\overline{9}$ $\overline{23}$

WHO IS THE ANGEL OF THE LORD?

$\overline{17}$ $\overline{22}$ $\overline{8}$ $\overline{6}$ $\overline{8}$

WHO IS JESUS?

$\overline{20}$ $\overline{12}$ $\overline{23}$

ANSWERS: THE ANGEL OF THE LORD, JESUS, GOD

135

UNSCRAMBLE THE LETTERS
OF THESE BOOKS OF THE BIBLE

CTUSLEIVI O _ _ _ O _ _ _ _

YONEUTERDMO _ _ _ O _ _ _ _ _ _ _

DJGUES _ _ O _ _ _

1KGINS _ _ _ _ _ O

NSIGK 2 _ _ _ _ _ _

NSICOECHRL _ _ _ _ _ _ _ _ O _

AERZ _ _ _ O

HNAEIHME O _ _ _ _ _ _ _

REESHT _ _ O _ _ _

OJB _ _ _

SPMSLA _ _ O _ O

SPBRREVO _ _ _ _ O _ _ _

PUT THE CIRCLED LETTERS IN THE RIGHT ORDER.
YOU'LL FIND THESE BOOKS OF THE BIBLE IN THE:

O O O   O O O O O O O   O O O.

ANSWERS: LEVITICUS, DEUTERONOMY, JUDGES, 1 KINGS, 2 KINGS, CHRONICLES, EZRA, NEHEMIAH, ESTHER, JOB, PSALMS, PROVERBS

ANSWER: OLD TESTAMENT

USE THE CODE BELOW TO ANSWER THE QUESTIONS.

A	B	C	D	E	F	G	H	I	J	K	L	M
26	25	24	23	22	21	20	19	18	17	16	15	14

N	O	P	Q	R	S	T	U	V	W	X	Y	Z
13	12	11	10	9	8	7	6	5	4	3	2	1

NAME THE BOOK THAT COMES
AFTER PSALMS.

‾11‾ ‾9‾ ‾12‾ ‾5‾ ‾22‾ ‾9‾ ‾25‾ ‾8‾

WHO WROTE MOST OF THE
BOOK OF PROVERBS?

‾16‾ ‾18‾ ‾13‾ ‾20‾

‾8‾ ‾12‾ ‾15‾ ‾12‾ ‾14‾ ‾12‾ ‾13‾

ANSWERS: PROVERBS, KING SOLOMON

137

LOOK IN YOUR BIBLE
LOOKS LIKE DANIEL IS IN A LOT OF DANGER!
FIND OUT WHAT HAPPENS -- THEN COLOR THE PICTURE.

READ DANIEL 6:1-24.

THESE THREE WERE PUT INTO A FIERY FURNACE BY KING NEBUCHADNEZZAR — BUT THEY WEREN'T EVEN SINGED!

WHO WERE THEY? USE THE CODE BELOW TO FIND OUT.

```
A  B  C  D  E  F
1  2  3  4  5  6
G  H  I  J  K  L
7  8  9  10 11 12
M  N  O  P  Q  R
13 14 15 16 17 18
S  T  U  V
19 20 21 22
W  X  Y  Z
23 24 25 26
```

___ ___ ___ ___ ___ ___ ___ ___ ,
19 8   1   4   18 1   3   8

___ ___ ___ ___ ___ ___ ___   AND   ___ ___ ___ ___ ___ ___ ___ ___
13 5   19 8   1   3   8   1   2   5   4   14 7   15

(GOOD LUCK PRONOUNCING THESE !!)

139

WHAT IS DAVID DOING?

TO FIND OUT, LOOK AT EACH LETTER
AND WRITE THE ONE THAT COMES
AFTER IT IN THE ALPHABET.

V Q H S H M F

O R * K L R

```
* A B C D E F G H I
  J K L M N O P Q R
  S T U V W X Y Z
```

ANSWER: WRITING PSALMS

140

WHAT IS A PSALM?

CROSS OUT EVERY LETTER THAT APPEARS FOUR TIMES IN THE PUZZLE. COPY THE REST OF THE LETTERS, IN ORDER, TO FIND THE ANSWER.

```
A D S P F C
F C P D O A
C N A C F D
P D F A G P
```

A PSALM IS A _____ .

READ PSALM 23, THEN DRAW YOURSELF INTO THE PICTURE

SOLVE THE PUZZLE

_ESSE   DAVID'S FATHER
₁

PHILISTIN_S   ISRAEL'S ENEMY
₂

_AUL   KING OF ISRAEL
₃

M_SIC   DAVID USES THIS TO COMFORT SAUL
₄

_AMUEL   GOD'S PROPHET
₅

_SRAEL   GOD'S NATION
₆

_ONS OF JESSE   DAVID'S BROTHERS
₇

_ORD   GOD
₈

G_LIATH   GIANT PHILISTINE
₉

WA_   ISRAEL FIGHTS
₁₀

_AVID   GOD'S NEW KING
₁₁

WHAT DOES IT SAY?

__ __ __ __ __ __ __ __ __ __ __
1   2   3   4   5   6   7   8   9   10   11

WORD JUMBLE

O P H ◯◯

P T E S ◯ ◯

Y R D ◯

HOW DAVID FLED FROM JERUSALEM

ON HIS ◯◯◯◯◯

USE THE CODE BELOW TO FIND THE NAMES OF JESUS' EARTHLY PARENTS.

A	B	C	D	E	F	G
26	25	24	23	22	21	20

H	I	J	K	L	M	N
19	18	17	16	15	14	13

O	P	Q	R	S	T	U
12	11	10	9	8	7	6

V	W	X	Y	Z
5	4	3	2	1

___ ___ ___ ___
14   26   9   2

AND

___ ___ ___ ___ ___ ___
17   12   8   22   11   19

JESUS AT THE TEMPLE

HOW OLD WAS JESUS THE FIRST TIME HE WENT TO THE TEMPLE? LOOK AT THE NUMBERED BRICKS, AND SOLVE THE QUESTION BELOW.

▭ + ▭ + ▭ + △ + ◇ + ▭ + ◇ + ▭ = ___

CHECK LUKE 2:41-52 TO MAKE SURE YOU HAVE THE RIGHT ANSWER

145

USE THE CODE BELOW TO FIND OUT WHAT JESUS
SAID TO DRIVE AWAY SATAN'S TEMPTATIONS.

IT IS
WRITTEN!

A B C D E F G
1 2 3 4 5 6 7
H I J K L M N
8 9 10 11 12 13 14
O P Q R S T U
15 16 17 18 19 20 21
V W X Y Z
22 23 24 25 26

1. ___ ___ ___   ___ ___ ___ ___   ___ ___ ___   ___ ___ ___ ___   ___ ___
   13 1 14   4 15 5 19   14 15 20   12 9 22 5   15 14

   ___ ___ ___ ___ ___   ___ ___ ___ ___ ___
   2 18 5 1 4   1 12 15 14 5

2. ___ ___   ___ ___ ___   ___ ___ ___   ___ ___ ___   ___ ___ ___ ___   ___ ___ ___ ___
   4 15   14 15 20   16 21 20   20 8 5   12 15 18 4   25 15 21 18

   ___ ___ ___   ___ ___ ___   ___ ___ ___   ___ ___ ___ ___
   7 15 4   20 15   20 8 5   20 5 19 20

3. ___ ___ ___ ___ ___ ___ ___ ___   ___ ___ ___   ___ ___ ___ ___   ___ ___ ___ ___ ___
   23 15 18 19 8 9 16   20 8 5   12 15 18 4   25 15 21 18

   ___ ___ ___   ___ ___ ___   ___ ___ ___ ___ ___   ___ ___ ___   ___ ___ ___ ___ ___
   7 15 4   1 14 4   19 5 18 22 5   8 9 13   15 14 12 25

JESUS HAS A MESSAGE FOR YOU.

UNSCRAMBLE THE WORDS, THEN PUT THE LETTERS IN THE MATCHING SHAPES BELOW.

SJESU   — ♡ — — —

HTTRU   — — ☆ — —

YWA   — — ◯

ELIF   — ▢ — —

NSI   — — —

YHOL   — △ ○ —

EVLO   — — ◇ —

DLRO   — △ — —

▢ ◯ △ ◇ ♡ ◯ △ ☆ .

WHAT'S JESUS DOING?

ADD OR SUBTRACT THE PICTURE CLUES AND LETTERS ACCORDING TO THE + OR − SIGNS TO FIND THE ANSWER.

− AT + E = _____

− P,G + S = _____

T + − C,H + ING = _____

− E = _____

− UM + 1 − NE + D = _____

148

UNSCRAMBLE THE LETTERS TO FIND OUT THE
NAMES OF SOME OF JESUS' DISCIPLES.
(HINT: LOOK UP MATTHEW 10:2-4.)

LIPPHI _____

STHOAM _____

MAJSE _____

THRABOOLMEW _____

NSMIO _____

SUJDA _____

TRPEE _____

NJHO _____

WHO THOUGHT HE WAS JESUS' FAVORITE
DISCIPLE?

ADD AND SUBTRACT THE PICTURE CLUES AND LETTERS.

 — ACK = ____

 — P,OL = ____

 — ORSE = ____

— ET = ____

ANSWER: JOHN

150

USE THE CODE BELOW TO FIND THE NAMES OF THE THREE
PERSONS OF THE TRINITY.

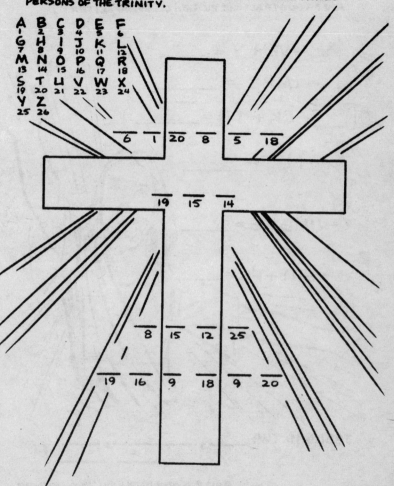

A 1	B 2	C 3	D 4	E 5	F 6
G 7	H 8	I 9	J 10	K 11	L 12
M 13	N 14	O 15	P 16	Q 17	R 18
S 19	T 20	U 21	V 22	W 23	X 24
Y 25	Z 26				

__6_ __1_ __20_ __8_ __5_ __18_

__19_ __15_ __14_

__8_ __15_ __12_ __25_

__19_ __16_ __9_ __18_ __9_ __20_

ADD OR SUBTRACT THE PICTURE CLUES AND LETTERS.

— VE + Y = _____

— IMBL = _____

— CK + TH = _____

— H = _____

— UMB + E = _____

— GHT + FE = _____

JESUS IS THE _____, ___ _____, _____ ___ ____!

USING THE CODE BELOW, FIND THE ANSWERS AND FINISH THE SENTENCES.

A	B	C	D	E	F	G	H	I	J	K	L	M
26	25	24	23	22	21	20	19	18	17	16	15	14

N	O	P	Q	R	S	T	U	V	W	X	Y	Z
13	12	11	10	9	8	7	6	5	4	3	2	1

THE BOOK OF ACTS TELLS WHAT HAPPENED TO $\underline{}\ \underline{}\ \underline{}\ \underline{}\ \underline{}$'
17 22 8 6 8

$\underline{}\ \underline{}\ \underline{}\ \underline{}\ \underline{}\ \underline{}\ \underline{}\ \underline{}\ \underline{}$ AFTER HIS RESURRECTION.
21 12 15 15 12 4 22 9 8

PETER WAS USED BY GOD TO $\underline{}\ \underline{}\ \underline{}\ \underline{}\ \underline{}\ \underline{}\ \underline{}\ \underline{}$
25 6 18 15 23 7 19 22

$\underline{}\ \underline{}\ \underline{}\ \underline{}\ \underline{}\ \underline{}$.
24 19 6 9 24 19

THE $\underline{}\ \underline{}\ \underline{}\ \underline{}\ \underline{}\ \underline{}$ $\underline{}\ \underline{}\ \underline{}\ \underline{}\ \underline{}\ \underline{}\ \underline{}$
20 12 8 11 22 15   12 21 24 19 9 18 8 7

SPREAD ALL OVER THE WORLD.

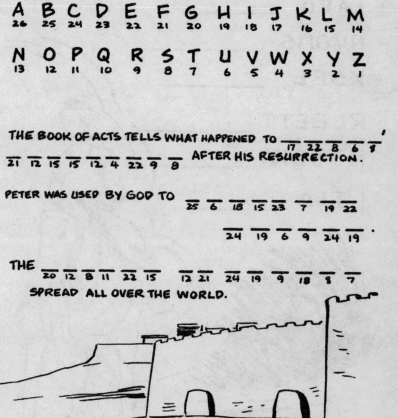

ANSWERS: JESUS, FOLLOWERS, BUILD THE CHURCH, GOSPEL OF CHRIST

153

UNSCRAMBLE THE WORDS

LAPU ________

NVOIIS ________

KSEE ________

RLEETT ________

HJSEIW ________

LJIA ________

ANSWERS: PAUL, VISION, SEEK, LETTER, JEWISH, JAIL

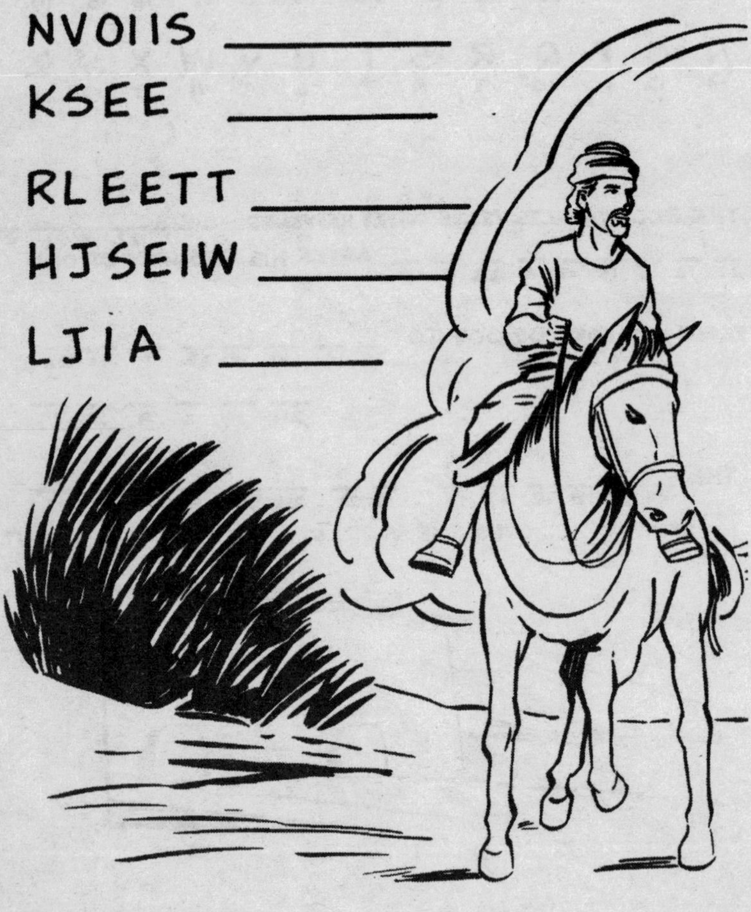

ADD OR SUBTRACT THE PICTURE
CLUES AND LETTERS.

IN THE BOOK OF ACTS, SAUL'S NAME WAS CHANGED TO

$- IG =$ _____

$- PPLE =$ _____

$- SA, CER =$ _____

$- BIB, E =$ _____

155

DID YOU KNOW?
ADD OR SUBTRACT THE PICTURE CLUES AND LETTERS.

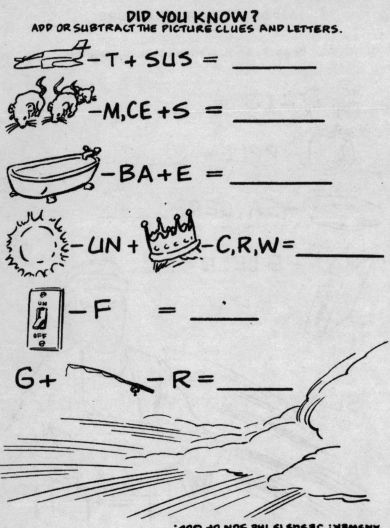

– T + SUS = _____

– M,CE + S = _____

– BA + E = _____

– UN + – C,R,W = _____

– F = ___

G + – R = _____

MATCH THE COLUMNS.

ANGEL

SPEAR

BRIDLE

TOUNGES OF
     FIRE

CHAINS

SLING

ARK

MATCH THE COLUMNS

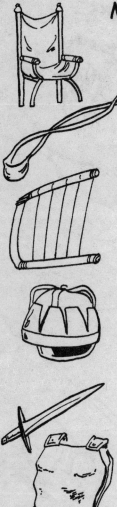

HARP

CROWN

THRONE

ARMOR

SLING

SWORD

MATCH THE COLUMNS

THORNS

PALM BRANCH

PIG

COLT

THE WORD

MATCH THE COLUMNS

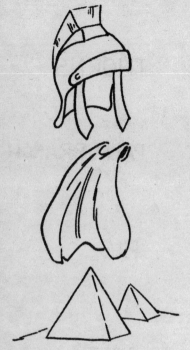

PYRAMID

PALM TREE

HELMET

SWORD

CLOAK

MATCH THE COLUMNS

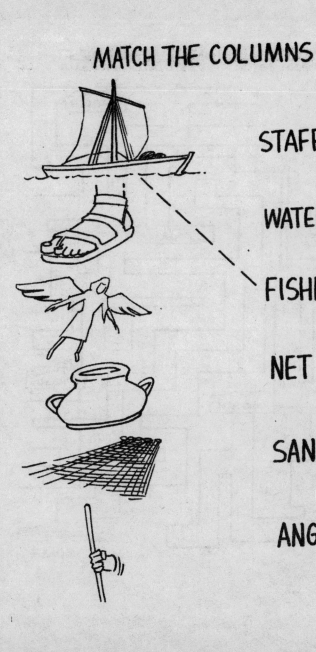

STAFF

WATER JUG

FISHING BOAT

NET

SANDAL

ANGEL

PAUL'S MISSIONARY JOURNEY
HELP PAUL GET TO HIS DESTINATION OF ROME.

JESUS WAS ARRESTED IN THE GARDEN OF GETHSEMANE. PETER TRIED TO GET AWAY FROM THE SOLDIERS. HELP HIM FIND HIS WAY OUT.

EXIT

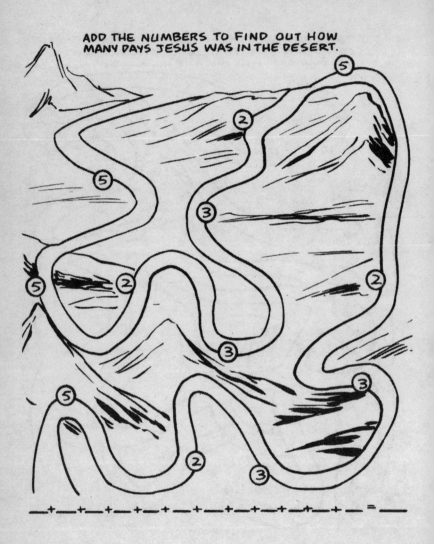

ADD THE NUMBERS TO FIND OUT HOW MANY DAYS JESUS WAS IN THE DESERT.

___ + ___ + ___ + ___ + ___ + ___ + ___ + ___ + ___ + ___ + ___ + ___ = ___

AS YOU GO THROUGH THE MAZE, PICK UP EACH LETTER AND FIND THE
ONLY WAY WE GET TO HEAVEN.

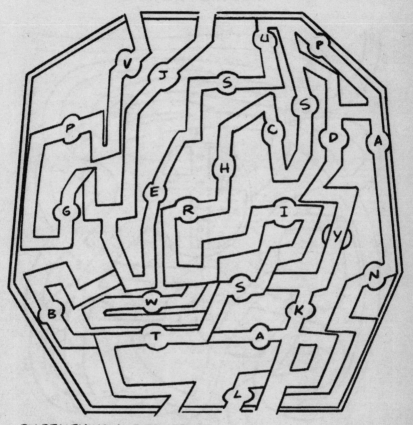

BY BELIEVING AND TRUSTING
IN: _____ ALONE!

MANY PATHS THAT LEAD NOWHERE - ONLY ONE SURE WAY.
CAN YOU FIND IT?

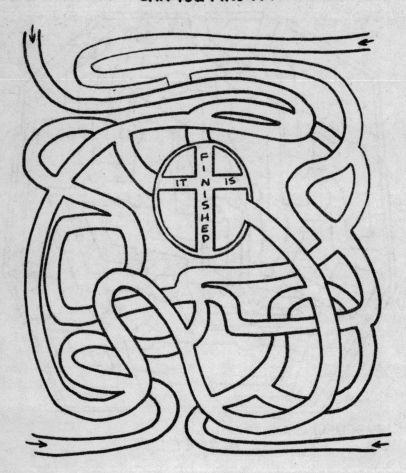

DANIEL AND THE ISRAELITES WERE TAKEN AS PRISONERS
OF WAR TO BABYLON — A BIG AND BUSY CITY.
HELP DANIEL FIND HIS NEW APARTMENT.

HELP THE ISRAELITES GET TO THE PROMISED LAND.

JOSEPH WAS SOLD AS A SLAVE BY HIS BROTHERS AND
TAKEN TO EGYPT. HELP THE CARAVAN GET THROUGH
THE DUNES AND AROUND THE DANGERS.

HELP DAVID ESCAPE SAUL

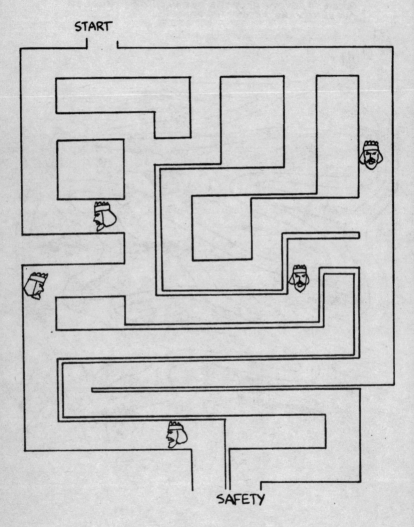

HELP DAVID GET OUT OF JERUSALEM

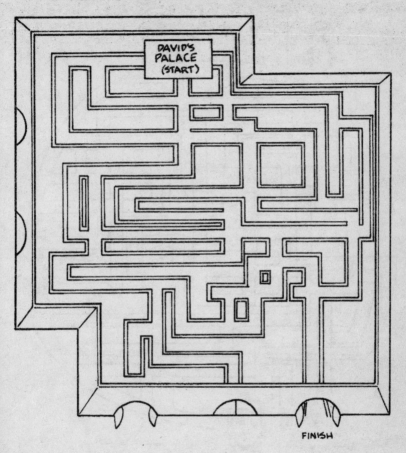

HELP SAMUEL FIND THE SON OF JESSE THAT GOD HAS CHOSEN

JESSE'S SONS

DAVID

ON TO JERUSALEM !

START

FINISH

HELP JOSEPH, MARY AND JESUS FIND THE WAY TO EGYPT

HOW TO DRAW DAVID

START WITH SIMPLE SHAPES

DRAW GUIDELINES <u>LIGHTLY</u>

DRAW DETAILS

FINISH AND ERASE GUIDELINES

NOW- TRY ON YOUR OWN PIECE OF PAPER!

175

HOW TO DRAW JESUS

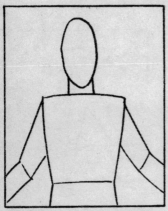

START WITH SIMPLE SHAPES

DRAW GUIDELINES <u>LIGHTLY</u>

ADD DETAILS: EYES, NOSE
MOUTH, EARS, BEARD,
HAIR AND CLOTHING

FINISH AND ERASE GUIDELINES

NOAH BUILT THE ARK

PUT THE PICTURES IN ORDER AS THEY HAPPENED FIRST,
SECOND, THIRD AND LAST. WRITE THE CORRECT NUMBER
IN THE BLANK SPACE UNDER EACH PICTURE.

\#_____

\#_____

\#_____

\#_____

ANSWER: 3, 2, 1, 4

177

ABRAM IS MOVING
GOD HAS TOLD ABRAM TO MOVE BY FAITH.
WHAT WILL HE TAKE WITH HIM?

COLOR ABRAM AND THE CORRECT ITEMS.

JOSEPH WAS GIVEN A COAT OF MANY COLORS.
USE THE COLOR GUIDE BELOW TO COLOR IT YOURSELF.

1=RED   2= YELLOW   3= BLUE   4= GREEN   5=ORANGE   6=PURPLE

FIND THE DIFFERENCES

MOSES COMES DOWN THE MOUNTAIN WITH THE TEN COMMANDMENTS OF GOD. CIRCLE THE DIFFERENCES.

SNAKES IN THE DESERT

CIRCLE THE SEVEN DEADLY SNAKES.

FIND THE DIFFERENCES

FIND THE DIFFERENCES

SOLOMON'S TEMPLE

JESUS IN THE MANGER

WHAT'S WRONG WITH THIS PICTURE?

ZACCHEUS, A WEALTHY TAX COLLECTOR, CLIMBED A TREE TO GET A BETTER LOOK AT JESUS. BUT, THIS IS A VERY STRANGE TREE. FIND AND CIRCLE WHAT DOESN'T BELONG.

FIND ALL THE BREAD AND FISH

FIND THE DIFFERENCES

WHAT'S WRONG WITH THIS PICTURE?

JESUS HAD FIVE THOUSAND PEOPLE TO FEED. ONLY TWO OF THE ITEMS BELOW ARE WHAT HE USED TO MULTIPLY WITH A MIRACLE. CIRCLE WHAT BELONGS.

ANSWER: HE USED THE BREAD AND FISHES

188

PETER'S GONE FISHING AND HIS NET IS FULL — BUT SOME OF HIS CATCH, HE COULD NOT SELL AT THE FISH MARKET! CIRCLE WHAT DOESN'T BELONG.

HELP PETER FIND HIS SHADOW.

PETER'S IN JAIL
FOR TALKING ABOUT JESUS!
BUT GOD HAS SENT AN ANGEL TO SET HIM FREE.
WHICH ONE IS THE ANGEL OF GOD?
COLOR HIM AND PETER.

191

FIND THE DIFFERENCES
PAUL ON HIS JOURNEY

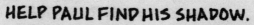

DRESS DAVID FOR BATTLE

WHAT BELONGS?

CUT OUT AND GLUE OR DRAW IT ON

DRAW MOSES

USING THE LEFT SIDE AS A GUIDE, DRAW, THEN COLOR, MOSES.

FINISH THE PICTURE
THEN
LOOK IN YOUR BIBLE.

THIS MAN WITH THE JAWBONE – DO YOU KNOW WHO HE IS?
HIS NAME IS _____ .

LOOK IN JUDGES 15: 15-16 FOR THE ANSWER.

DRAW FOR YOURSELF

FINISH THE OTHER SIDE.

DRAW FOR YOURSELF

USING WHAT IS IN EACH SQUARE, GO TO THE FOLLOWING
PAGE AND COPY THIS PICTURE.

COPY FROM THE PREVIOUS PAGE.

DRAW FOR YOURSELF

USING THE SQUARES AS A GUIDE, GO TO THE FOLLOWING PAGE
AND COPY THIS PICTURE.

200

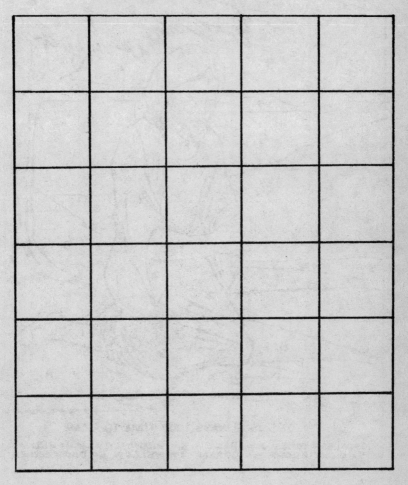

COLOR BY NUMBER

JESUS ALWAYS TOOK TIME TO PRAY

1= FLESH TONE 2 = BLUE 3 = BROWN 4= LIGHT BLUE
5= LIGHT BROWN 6= GREEN 7 = YELLOW 8= DARK GREEN
9= GREY

FINISH THE PICTURE
JESUS DIED ON A CROSS FOR OUR SINS.

FINISH THE PICTURE

THEN COLOR.

204

Answer Pages

FIND THE WORDS BELOW IN THE WORDSEARCH PUZZLE.

ETERNAL		HIM
WORLD		LIFE
SON		BELIEVES
PERISH		HIS
GOD		LOVED

3

"FOR GOD SO LOVED THE WORLD..."

FINISH THE PICTURE.

4

FIND THE WORDS TO THIS VERSE IN THE WORDSEARCH BELOW

"FOR ALL HAVE SINNED AND FALL SHORT OF THE GLORY OF GOD."

ROMANS 3:23

5

FIND THE WORDS TO THIS VERSE IN THE WORDSEARCH BELOW

"WHILE WE WERE STILL SINNERS CHRIST DIED FOR US"

ROMANS 5:8

6

7

USE THE CODE CHART TO MATCH THE NUMBERS WITH LETTERS. USE THE COLUMN GOING DOWN, FIRST, THEN WRITE THE LETTERS IN THE BLANKS.

	1	2	3	4	5	6
1	A	F	K	P	U	Z
2	B	G	L	Q	V	
3	C	H	M	R	W	
4	D	I	N	S	X	
5	E	J	O	T	Y	

"FOR THE WAGES OF
SIN IS DEATH, BUT
THE GIFT OF GOD
IS ETERNAL LIFE
IN CHRIST JESUS
OUR LORD."

Romans 6:23

8

CONNECT THE DOTS

9

TRAVEL THE PATH THAT MAKES A SENTENCE

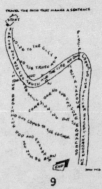

START ... END

John 14:6

10

AFTER GOING THROUGH THE MAZE ON THE PREVIOUS PAGE, FILL IN THE BLANKS BELOW TO FINISH THE SENTENCE.

"I AM THE WAY AND THE
TRUTH AND THE LIFE.
NO ONE COMES TO
THE FATHER EXCEPT
THROUGH ME."

John 14:6

NOW FIND THE UNDERLINED WORDS IN THE WORD SEARCH BELOW:

11

USE THE CODE CHART TO MATCH THE NUMBERS WITH LETTERS. USE THE COLUMN GOING DOWN, FIRST, THEN WRITE THE LETTERS IN THE BLANKS.

	1	2	3	4	5	6
1	A	F	K	P	U	Z
2	B	G	L	Q	V	
3	C	H	M	R	W	
4	D	I	N	S	X	
5	E	J	O	T	Y	

John 5:24

"I TELL YOU THE
TRUTH, WHOEVER
HEARS MY WORD
AND BELIEVES
HIM WHO SENT ME
HAS ETERNAL
LIFE AND WILL NOT
BE CONDEMNED."

12

FINISH THE PICTURE OF JESUS.

13

TRAVEL THE PATH THAT MAKES A SENTENCE.

START ... END

Romans 10:9

14

AFTER GOING THROUGH THE MAZE ON THE PREVIOUS PAGE, FILL IN THE BLANKS BELOW TO FINISH THE SENTENCE.

"IF YOU CONFESS
WITH YOUR MOUTH,
'JESUS IS LORD,' AND
BELIEVE IN YOUR
HEART THAT GOD
RAISED HIM FROM
THE DEAD, YOU WILL BE
SAVED."

Romans 10:9

15

FIND THE WORDS BELOW IN THE WORDSEARCH PUZZLE.

LORD	RAISED
HEART	MOUTH
DEAD	BELIEVE
CONFESS	JESUS
SAVED	

16

COLOR THE PICTURE

16

17

JESUS IS KNOCKING AT THE DOOR OF
YOUR HEART. WHAT SHOULD YOU DO?

USE THE CODE CHART BELOW TO MATCH
THE CODES WITH LETTERS. USE THE
COLUMN GOING DOWN FIRST, THEN
WRITE THE LETTERS IN THE BLANKS
TO COMPLETE THE VERSE.

THEN YOU WILL KNOW WHAT TO DO!

	1	2	3	4	5	6	7
1	A	H	I	P	Q	X	Y
2	B	G	J	O	R	W	Z
3	C	F	K	N	S	V	
4	D	E	L	M	T	U	

"HERE AM I. I STAND
AT THE DOOR AND
KNOCK."

CONTINUED NEXT PAGE.

17

18

CONTINUED FROM PREVIOUS PAGE

	1	2	3	4	5	6	7
1	A	H	I	P	Q	X	Y
2	B	G	J	O	R	W	Z
3	C	F	K	N	S	V	
4	D	E	L	M	T	U	

"IF ANYONE HEARS
MY VOICE AND
OPENS THE DOOR,
I WILL COME IN
AND EAT WITH
HIM AND HE WITH
ME."

REVELATION 3:20

18

19

19

20

DO YOU KNOW JESUS LOVES YOU? DO
YOU KNOW HOW MUCH JESUS LOVES YOU?
HE LOVES YOU SO MUCH THAT HE DIED
TO PAY THE PRICE FOR YOUR SIN. THERE
IS ONLY ONE SIN THAT GOD WILL NOT
FORGIVE. THAT SIN IS NOT BELIEVING
IN JESUS AND WHAT HE DID FOR YOU AND
ALL OF US. WITHOUT JESUS, WITHOUT
ACCEPTING THAT HE DIED FOR US, NO ONE
CAN GO TO HEAVEN.

THREE DAYS AFTER JESUS DIED, HE WAS
RAISED TO NEW LIFE. HE WANTS TO SHARE
THAT WITH US TOO! HE WANTS TO GIVE US
NEW LIFE ... ETERNAL LIFE!

DO YOU WANT TO ASK JESUS TO COME
INTO YOUR HEART AND YOUR LIFE? ALL
YOU NEED TO DO IS ASK HIM. YOU
COULD SAY A PRAYER LIKE THIS:

DEAR JESUS,

I KNOW I AM A SINNER AND THAT
YOU DIED FOR ALL MY SINS. I KNOW
YOU ROSE FROM THE DEAD. JESUS,
I ASK YOU NOW TO COME INTO MY
HEART AND TAKE CONTROL OF MY
LIFE.
THANK YOU FOR ALL YOU HAVE DONE
FOR ME.
TEACH ME YOUR WAYS, JESUS, AND
HELP ME TO GROW UP WITH YOU.

IN JESUS' NAME, I PRAY. AMEN.

IF YOU HAVE NEVER INVITED JESUS
INTO YOUR HEART AND LIFE BUT YOU
WANT TO NOW, GO TO THE NEXT PAGE AND
WRITE OUT YOUR PRAYER IN YOUR OWN
WORDS. JUST TELL JESUS HOW YOU REALLY
FEEL.

20

21

MY VERY OWN PRAYER TO INVITE
JESUS INTO MY HEART AND LIFE

DATE :

DEAR LORD JESUS,

_____
_____
_____
_____
_____
_____
_____
_____

IN JESUS' NAME, AMEN.

_____
YOUR NAME

21

22

DID YOU INVITE JESUS INTO YOUR HEART?
FIND YOUR WAY TO JESUS!

22

23

WOW! IF YOU ASKED JESUS INTO
YOUR LIFE, YOU ARE NOW A CHRISTIAN!
YOU ARE NOW A CHILD OF GOD!

LET'S LEARN HOW TO GET TO KNOW
JESUS BETTER.

UNSCRAMBLE THE WORDS BELOW TO
FIND OUT HOW TO BEGIN.

1) TO BECOME A CHILD OF GOD, YOU HAD
   TO ASK JESUS INTO YOUR HEART. THIS
   IS CALLED _____
   IYGNRAP

2) PRAYING IS _____ WITH GOD.
   ATINALK

3) JUST LIKE YOU TALK WITH YOUR MOM
   OR DAD, GOD WANTS YOU TO _____
   WITH HIM.   TWNAS   KTLA

4) IT DOES NOT STOP THERE. GOD WANTS
   TO TALK TO YOU! JESUS SPEAKS TO YOU
   THROUGH HIS _____
   DRWO

5) THE ONLY WAY TO REALLY KNOW JESUS
   IS TO _____ ABOUT _____
   ARDE   IHM

6) WE READ ABOUT _____ IN THE HOLY
   _____.   JSSUE
   EBLIB

23

24

IN THE FOLLOWING WORDSEARCH PUZZLE,
FIND AND CIRCLE THE WORDS LISTED.

THEY CAN BE FOUND IN LINES GOING
FORWARD, BACKWARD, UP, DOWN, OR
DIAGONALLY.

LOVED	HEARS	EAT
KNOCK	VOICE	ANYONE
DOOR	HIM	STAND

24

WHAT HAVE YOU LEARNED ABOUT
BEING A CHILD OF GOD?

FIND AND CIRCLE THE WORDS LISTED
BELOW.

PRAY WORD TALK
READ JESUS GOD
BIBLE SAVIOUR INVITE

25

CONNECT THE DOTS
AND FINISH THE PHRASE.

JESUS, THE L I O N OF JUDAH!

26

ACROSS

1. GOD **GAVE** US HIS ONE AND ONLY SON.

2. NOW WE CAN HAVE ETERNAL **LIFE**.

3. JESUS KNOCKS AT THE DOORS OF
   OUR **HEARTS**.

4. IF WE HAVE **JESUS** IN HIM N, WE
   WILL NEVER LEAVE US.

DOWN

5. WE ARE NOW A CHILD OF **GOD**.

6. WE TALK TO HIM BY **PRAYING**.

7. HE TALKS TO US THROUGH **HIS**
   WORD.

8. HIS WORD IS THE **BIBLE**.

WORD LIST

PRAYING	HEARTS
LIFE	BIBLE
GAVE	HIS
INVITED	GOD

27

28

SOMETIMES, IT'S NOT EASY TO READ THE
BIBLE EVERY DAY. OTHER THINGS
WILL TRY TO GET IN THE WAY, BUT IF YOU
REALLY WANT TO GROW AS A CHRISTIAN, IT IS
BEST TO READ IN GOD'S WORD EACH DAY.

FIND YOUR WAY TO THE BIBLE.

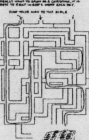

29

TRACE THE PATH THAT MAKES A SENTENCE.

JOHN 15:26

30

AFTER GOING THROUGH THE MAZE ON
THE PREVIOUS PAGE, FILL IN THE BLANKS
BELOW TO FINISH THE SENTENCE.

"WHEN THE C O U N S E L O R
COMES, W H O M I WILL
S E N D TO Y O U FROM THE
F A T H E R, THE S P I R I T
OF T R U T H WHO G O E S
OUT FROM THE FATHER, HE
WILL T E S T I F Y
A B O U T ME."   JOHN 15:26

31

FIND THE WORDS BELOW IN THE
WORDSEARCH PUZZLE.

SPIRIT WHOM YOU
ABOUT TRUTH TESTIFY
GOES COUNSELOR SEND

32

COLOR THE PICTURE

WHEN YOU BECOME A CHILD OF GOD,
WHERE DOES THE HOLY SPIRIT LIVE?

GO ON TO THE NEXT PAGE TO FIND
THE ANSWER.

33

USE THE CODE CHART BELOW TO MATCH THE CODES WITH LETTERS. USE THE COLUMN GOING DOWN, FIRST, THEN WRITE THE LETTERS IN THE BLANKS.

	1	2	3	4	5	6	7
1	A	I	J	F	Q	X	V
2	B	G	J	O	R	W	Z
3	C	F	K	N	S	U	Y
4	U	E	L	M	T	D	!

"DO YOU NOT KNOW
THAT YOUR BODY
IS A TEMPLE OF
THE HOLY SPIRIT,
WHO IS IN YOU,
WHOM YOU HAVE
RECEIVED FROM GOD."
1 Corinthians 6:19

34

THE HOLY SPIRIT ACTUALLY COMES TO LIVE INSIDE YOU ! YOUR BODY BECOMES THE TEMPLE, OR DWELLING PLACE OF GOD'S SPIRIT.

THIS IS HARD TO UNDERSTAND BECAUSE WE CAN'T SEE HIM, BUT IT IS TRUE. BECAUSE THE BIBLE SAYS IT IS SO. MANY TIMES THE HOLY SPIRIT MAKES HIS PRESENCE KNOWN. WE CAN FEEL HIM AS HE GIVES US HIS POWER AND STRENGTH TO LIVE AS GOD WANTS US TO LIVE.

CONNECT THE DOTS

35

ONCE, OUR HUMAN SPIRITS WERE DEAD. WE WERE BORN SPIRITUALLY DEAD. JESUS GIVES US NEW LIFE IN OUR SPIRITS !

"FOR JUST AS THE FATHER RAISES THE DEAD AND GIVES THEM LIFE, EVEN SO THE SON GIVES LIFE TO WHOM HE IS PLEASED TO GIVE IT."
John 5:21

GO TO THE NEXT PAGE. USING THE GRID, DRAW THE ABOVE PICTURE FOR YOURSELF.

36

FROM THE PREVIOUS PAGE, USE THE GRID TO DRAW THE PICTURE FOR YOURSELF.

37

NOW THAT YOU ARE A CHRISTIAN, YOU MUST LET THE HOLY SPIRIT TEACH YOU HOW TO LIVE YOUR NEW LIFE. HOW DOES HE DO THIS?

USE THE CODE CHART BELOW TO MATCH THE CODES WITH LETTERS. USE THE COLUMN GOING DOWN, FIRST, THEN WRITE THE LETTERS IN THE BLANKS ON THE FOLLOWING PAGE.

	1	2	3	4	5	6	7
1	A	B	C	D	E	F	G
2	H	I	J	K	L	M	N
3	O	P	Q	R	S	T	U
4	V	W	X	Y	Z		

WHAT YOU PUT INTO YOUR MIND, WHAT YOU READ OR WATCH OR LISTEN TO IS WHAT WILL COME OUT OF YOU. IF YOU PUT GOD'S WORD IN, IF YOU READ THE BIBLE REGULARLY, GOD'S CHARACTER WILL COME OUT OF YOU IN THE WAYS YOU THINK, ACT AND THE CHOICES YOU MAKE.

38

USING THE CODE CHART FROM THE PREVIOUS PAGE, COMPLETE THE VERSE BELOW.

"DO NOT CONFORM
ANY LONGER TO THE
PATTERN OF THIS
WORLD, BUT BE
TRANSFORMED BY
THE RENEWING
OF YOUR MIND."
Romans 12:2

39

COLOR THE PICTURE

BE CAREFUL IN YOUR CHOICES!

40

TRAVEL THE PATH THAT MAKES A SENTENCE.

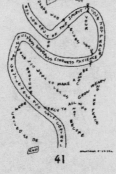

41

AFTER GOING THROUGH THE MAZE ON THE PREVIOUS PAGE, FILL IN THE BLANKS BELOW TO FINISH THE VERSE.

"BUT THE FRUIT OF
THE SPIRIT IS
LOVE, JOY,
PEACE,
PATIENCE,
KINDNESS,
GOODNESS,
FAITHFULNESS,
GENTLENESS,
AND SELF-CONTROL"
Galatians 5:22, 23 a

42

FIND THE WORDS BELOW IN THE
WORDSEARCH PUZZLE.

JOY   KINDNESS
SELF-CONTROL   SPIRIT
GENTLENESS   PATIENCE
PEACE   GOODNESS
FRUIT   LOVE
FAITHFULNESS

43

THE FRUIT OF THE SPIRIT

FILL IN THE BLANKS

PATIENCE

GOODNESS

LOVE

FAITHFULNESS

SELF-CONTROL   PEACE

KINDNESS   JOY

GENTLENESS

44

YOU ALREADY KNOW THAT WHEN YOU
BECOME A CHRISTIAN, THE HOLY SPIRIT
COMES TO LIVE IN YOU. THE HOLY SPIRIT
WILL LEAD YOU INTO GOD'S TRUTH AND
HE WILL DO THE WORK OF PRODUCING
GOD'S CHARACTER IN YOU. IF YOU WILL
LET HIM. YOU CAN DO THIS BY CHOOSING
TO DO WHAT GOD WANTS RATHER THAN
WHAT YOU WANT. THIS IS CALLED
SURRENDERING, OR GIVING UP, TO GOD'S
WILL.

GOD'S CHARACTER IS THE FRUIT OF
THE SPIRIT.

UNSCRAMBLE THE WORDS BELOW TO
FIND GOD'S CHARACTER, THE FRUIT OF
THE SPIRIT.

OVLE	L O V E
OYJ	J O Y
PCEEA	P E A C E
TIEENCPA	P A T I E N C E
DNNESKSI	K I N D N E S S
OGOOSSNE	G O O D N E S S
HTAIFLUNFSES	F A I T H F U L N E S S
TNLEEEGSSN	G E N T L E N E S S
- RTNSCLEOLLO	S E L F - C O N T R O L

45

FIND YOUR WAY THROUGH THE
OBSTACLES. THE THINGS OF THIS WORLD,
THAT WILL TRY TO PULL YOU AWAY FROM
WHAT GOD WOULD WANT YOU TO DO

END

46

FINISH THE PICTURE

AS YOU START TO LIVE YOUR NEW LIFE AS
GOD'S CHILD, IT IS IMPORTANT TO KNOW
WHO YOUR ENEMIES ARE.

THE CHRISTIAN HAS THREE ENEMIES:
1. THE DEVIL
2. THE SINFUL NATURE (THE FLESH)
3. THE WORLD

A CHRISTIAN IN THIS WORLD IS LIKE A
SOLDIER — A SOLDIER OF THE LORD
YOUR ONLY WEAPON IS THE BIBLE

47

USE THE CODE CHART BELOW TO MATCH
THE CODES WITH LETTERS. USE THE
COLUMN GOING DOWN, FIRST, THEN
WRITE THE LETTERS IN THE BLANKS

	1	2	3	4	5	6	7
1	A	B	C	D	E	F	G
2	H	I	J	K	L	M	N
3	O	P	Q	R	S	T	U
4	V	W	X	Y	Z		

"BE SELF-CONTROLLED
AND ALERT YOUR
ENEMY THE DEVIL
PROWLS AROUND
LIKE A ROARING
LION LOOKING
FOR SOMEONE
TO DEVOUR"

48

OUR LORD NEVER LEAVES HIS CHILDREN
HELPLESS. HE ALWAYS GIVES US A WAY
TO STAND AGAINST OUR ENEMY THE
DEVIL.
TO FIND OUT HOW, USE THE CODE CHART BELOW
TO COMPLETE THE VERSE. USE THE COLUMNS
GOING DOWN FIRST.

	1	2	3	4	5	6	7
1	A	B	C	D	E	F	G
2	H	I	J	K	L	M	N
3	O	P	Q	R	S	T	U
4	V	W	X	Y	Z		

"SUBMIT YOUR
SELVES THEN TO
GOD RESIST
THE DEVIL,
AND HE WILL
FLEE FROM YOU"

JAMES 4:7

49

CONNECT-THE-DOTS

"... RESIST THE DEVIL, AND HE WILL FLEE..."

50

WANT TO YOU NEED TO DO WHEN THE
DEVIL TEMPTS YOU TO SIN?

AS YOU GO THROUGH THE MAZE, COLLECT
THE LETTERS AND COMPLETE THE
STATEMENT BELOW.

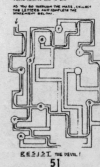

R E S I S T THE DEVIL!

51

52

WHAT IS THE DEVIL LIKE?

AS YOU GO THROUGH THE MAZE, COLLECT THE LETTERS AND COMPLETE THE STATEMENT BELOW.

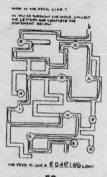

THE DEVIL IS LIKE A R O A R I N G LION!

53

PSALM 119: 104-105 GIVES ANOTHER DESCRIPTION OF GOD'S WORD, THE BIBLE. USE THIS CODE BELOW TO COMPLETE THESE TWO VERSES. USE THE COLUMNS GOING DOWN FIRST.

	1	2	3	4	5	6	7
1	A	B	C	D	E	F	G
2	H	I	J	K	L	M	N
3	O	P	Q	R	S	T	U
4	V	W	X	Y	Z		

54

THE BIBLE IS A LAMP THAT LIGHTS OUR WAY IN THE DARKNESS OF SIN AND TEMPTATION.

USING THE GRID, DRAW THE PICTURE BELOW ON THE NEXT PAGE

55

FROM THE PREVIOUS PAGE, USE THE GRID TO DRAW THE PICTURE FOR YOURSELF

56

THE SECOND ENEMY IN OUR WALK WITH THE LORD IS OUR SINFUL NATURE ALSO KNOWN AS THE "FLESH". THIS SINFUL NATURE OR FLESH IS A PART OF ALL OF US. WE ARE BORN WITH IT.

USE THE CODE CHART BELOW TO MATCH THE CODES WITH LETTERS. USE THE COLUMN GOING DOWN FIRST, THEN WRITE THE LETTERS IN THE BLANKS.

	1	2	3	4	5	6	7
4			Z	Y	X	W	V
3	O	P	Q	R	S	T	U
2	N	M	L	K	J	I	H
1	A	B	C	D	E	F	G

57

FIND THE WORDS BELOW IN THE WORDSEARCH PUZZLE.

WORSHIPING   ANGRY
ACTS   JEALOUSY
SINFUL   HATING
NATURE   LYING
FLESH   SHARING

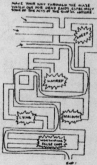

58

THE BIBLE TELLS US HOW TO FIGHT THE DESIRES OF THE SINFUL NATURE.

USE THE CODE CHART BELOW TO MATCH THE CODES WITH LETTERS. USE THE COLUMN GOING DOWN, FIRST, THEN WRITE THE LETTERS IN THE BLANKS.

	1	2	3	4	5	6	7
4			Z	Y	X	W	V
3	O	P	Q	R	S	T	U
2	N	M	L	K	J	I	H
1	A	B	C	D	E	F	G

59

FIND THE WORDS BELOW IN THE WORDSEARCH PUZZLE.

JESUS   STEP
SPIRIT   DESIRES
BELONG   KEEP
PASSIONS   CHRIST
CRUCIFIED   LIVE

60

MAKE YOUR WAY THROUGH THE MAZE WATCH OUT FOR DEAD ENDS ESPECIALLY SOME OF THE ACTS OF THE SINFUL NATURE.

FINISH THE FACE

YOU DO THE DRAWING! DRAW THE
EXPRESSION FOR JOY.

JOY - A FRUIT OF THE HOLY SPIRIT!

61

FINISH THE FACE

YOU DO THE DRAWING! DRAW THE
EXPRESSION FOR PEACE!

PEACE - A FRUIT OF THE HOLY SPIRIT!

62

FINISH THE FACE

YOU DO THE DRAWING! DRAW THE
EXPRESSION FOR LOVE.

LOVE - A FRUIT OF THE HOLY SPIRIT!

63

FINISH THE FACE

YOU DO THE DRAWING! DRAW THE
EXPRESSION FOR ANGER.

ANGER - AN ACT OF THE SINFUL NATURE.

64

FINISH THE FACE

YOU DO THE DRAWING! DRAW THE
EXPRESSION FOR HATRED!

HATRED - AN ACT OF THE SINFUL NATURE

65

THE THIRD ENEMY IN OUR LIVES WITH GOD
IS THE WORLD.

IT IS NOT THE WORLD IN ITSELF THAT IS
OUR ENEMY AS GOD CREATED THE WORLD.
IT IS SOME OF THE THINGS IN THE WORLD
THAT CAN LEAD US AWAY FROM GOD AND
WHAT HE WANTS US TO DO.

GO THROUGH THE MAZE.

66

CIRCLE THESE THINGS THAT COULD BE USED
TO TEMPT YOU TO SIN AND TAKE YOU AWAY
FROM GOD'S PLAN FOR YOUR LIFE
(YOU MAY BE SURPRISED!)

A LOT OF THINGS CAN
BE USED FOR BAD AS WELL
AS GOOD!

67

WHAT DOES GOD SAY ABOUT THE THINGS OF
THE WORLD?

USE THE CODE CHART BELOW TO MATCH
THE CODES WITH LETTERS. USE THE
COLUMN GOING DOWN FIRST THEN WRITE
THE LETTERS IN THE BLANKS.

"DO NOT LOVE THE
WORLD OR ANYTHING
IN THE WORLD. IF
ANYONE LOVES THE
WORLD, THE LOVE OF
THE FATHER IS NOT
IN HIM."

68

UNSCRAMBLE THE UNDERLINED WORDS
AND PLACE THEM IN THE CORRECT SPACE
IN THE CROSS WORD GRID IN THE NEXT PAGE.

ACROSS

1. THE HOLY SPIRIT WILL LEAD YOU INTO
ALL _THRUT_.

2. YOUR _BDYO_ IS THE TEMPLE OF THE
HOLY SPIRIT

3. YOU HAVE THREE ENEMIES. ONE OF THEM
IS THE _IVEEL_.

4. ANOTHER IS YOUR ENEMIES IS YOUR
FLESH OR THE SINFUL _AERTUN_.

DOWN

5. THE HOLY SPIRIT IS ALSO CALLED
THE _LORSECNOU_.

6. YOU ARE TO BE CHANGED BY THE
RENEWING OF YOUR _NMDI_.

7. THE HOLY SPIRIT WILL PRODUCE
GOD'S _TFIUR_ IN YOU.

8. YOUR THIRD ENEMY IS THE THINGS
OF THE _RWLDO_.

WORD LIST

MIND	DEVIL
BODY	NATURE
COUNSELOR	TRUTH
WORLD	FRUIT

69

70

EVEN THOUGH YOU ARE NOW GOD'S CHILD, YOU WILL STILL SIN! WANT TO GET BACK ON THE PATH? TRAVEL THE PATH THAT MAKES A SENTENCE

71

AFTER GOING THROUGH THE MAZE ON THE PREVIOUS PAGE, FILL IN THE BLANKS BELOW TO FINISH THE VERSE.

"IF WE <u>CONFESS</u> OUR SINS,
HE (GOD) IS <u>FAITHFUL</u> AND
<u>JUST</u> AND WILL <u>FORGIVE</u>
US OUR <u>SINS</u> AND <u>PURIFY</u> US
FROM ALL
<u>UNRIGHTEOUSNESS</u>."
1 JOHN 1:9

72

FIND THE WORDS BELOW IN THE
WORDSEARCH PUZZLE

FORGIVE   SINS

FAITHFUL   JUST

PURIFY   CONFESS

        UNRIGHTEOUSNESS

73

OUR LORD JESUS PAID THE PRICE FOR
OUR SINS. HE TOOK OUR PUNISHMENT
BY DYING ON THE CROSS.

USING THE GRID, DRAW THE PICTURE
BELOW ON THE NEXT PAGE

74

FROM THE PREVIOUS PAGE, USE THE
GRID TO DRAW THE PICTURE FOR YOURSELF

75

ALL CHRISTIANS ARE TEMPTED TO SIN,
TO DO THINGS THAT ARE WRONG. BUT WE
CAN TRUST GOD TO HELP US IN OUR
TIMES OF TEMPTATION

USE THE CODE CHART BELOW TO MATCH
THE CODES WITH LETTERS. LINE THE
COLUMN GOING DOWN, FIRST, THEN WRITE
THE LETTERS IN THE BLANKS.

	7	6	5	4	3	2	1
4	A	H	I	P	Q	X	Y
3	B	G	J	O	R	W	Z
2	C	F	K	N	S	V	
1	D	E	L	M	T	U	

"THE ONLY
TEMPTATIONS
THAT YOU HAVE
ARE THE
TEMPTATIONS
THAT ALL PEOPLE

CONT'D NEXT PAGE

76

CONT'D FROM PREVIOUS PAGE

HAVE. BUT YOU
CAN TRUST GOD.
HE WILL NOT LET
YOU BE TEMPTED
MORE THAN YOU
CAN STAND. BUT
WHEN YOU ARE,
GOD WILL ALSO
GIVE YOU A WAY
TO ESCAPE THAT
TEMPTATION.
THEN YOU WILL
BE ABLE TO
STAND IT."

1 CORINTHIANS 10:13
(SIMPLIFIED BIBLE)

77

CONNECT-THE-DOTS

FIGHTING TEMPTATION ON YOUR OWN

78

CONNECT-THE-DOTS

FIGHTING TEMPTATION WITH GOD!

79

SOMETIMES YOU MAY NOT FEEL LIKE YOU ARE A CHRISTIAN. YOU MAY EVEN WONDER IF JESUS REALLY DID COME INTO YOUR HEART.

ESPECIALLY IF YOU FEEL LIKE THIS WHEN YOU KEEP MAKING THE SAME MISTAKE OVER AND OVER, OR WHEN IT SEEMS LIKE YOU ARE ALWAYS TEMPTED TO DO WHAT YOU KNOW IS SIN.

JESUS NEVER LIES. THE BIBLE IS TRUE. IF YOU REALLY MEANT IT WHEN YOU ASKED JESUS INTO YOUR HEART, THEN YOU CAN BELIEVE THAT JESUS IS IN YOU.

THIS IS WHAT GOD'S WORD SAYS:

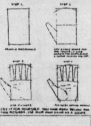

"I GIVE THEM ETERNAL LIFE,
AND THEY SHALL NEVER PERISH,
NO ONE CAN SNATCH THEM
OUT OF MY HAND."

JOHN 10:28

80

THE ONLY WAY TO HEAVEN IS THROUGH JESUS CHRIST. HAVING JESUS IN YOUR HEART MEANS YOU HAVE BEEN GIVEN ETERNAL LIFE, AND YOU WILL LIVE WITH GOD FOREVER. THIS IS GOD'S PROMISE TO YOU.

FIND THE UNDERLINED WORDS IN THE WORD SEARCH PUZZLE BELOW.

"I <u>GIVE</u> THEM <u>ETERNAL</u> <u>LIFE</u>, AND THEY <u>SHALL NEVER</u> <u>PERISH</u>; NO ONE CAN <u>SNATCH</u> THEM OUT OF MY <u>HAND</u>."

81

FROM THE START OF YOUR CHRISTIAN LIFE TO THE END OF IT, YOU WILL ALWAYS STAY IN THE HAND OF THE LORD JESUS.

LIFE WILL NOT ALWAYS BE EASY, BUT JESUS WILL GET YOU THROUGH!

FIND YOUR WAY THROUGH THE MAZE OF LIFE.

END

82

HOW TO DRAW THE HAND

STEP 1.   STEP 2.

STEP 3.   STEP 4.

TRY IT FOR YOURSELF. YOU MAY WANT TO USE YOUR OWN HAND AS A GUIDE.

83

UNSCRAMBLE THE UNDERLINED WORDS AND PLACE THEM IN THE CROSSWORD GRID ON THE NEXT PAGE.

ACROSS

1. WE ARE TO <u>SSFCNOE</u> OUR SINS TO GOD.

2. WE ARE ALL <u>PTMEDTE</u> TO SIN.

3. THE BIBLE SAYS THAT PEOPLE ARE LIKE <u>PEESH</u>.

4. NO ONE CAN <u>ASETL</u> US OUT OF GOD'S HAND.

DOWN

1. GOD WILL MAKE OUR HEARTS <u>CLNAE</u> AND NEW.

2. GOD WILL <u>EFGRVOI</u> US FOR OUR SINS.

3. THE TEMPTATIONS THAT COME ARE WHAT COME TO ALL <u>EEPOLP</u>.

4. GOD WILL GIVE US A WAY TO ESCAPE TEMPTATION SO WE CAN <u>ASDNT</u>.

WORD LIST

SHEEP	PEOPLE
STAND	FORGIVE
CONFESS	STEAL
TEMPTED	CLEAN

84

C O N F E S S
L
E
A
N
F O R G I V E
S
T
A
T E M P T E D
N
P
E
S H E E P O
P
L
E
S T E A L

85

IF YOU REMEMBER, WHEN YOU INVITE JESUS CHRIST INTO YOUR LIFE, YOUR BODY BECOMES THE TEMPLE OF GOD'S HOLY SPIRIT.

IN OTHER WORDS, YOUR BODY BECOMES THE "HOUSE" THAT THE HOLY SPIRIT DWELLS IN. AS YOU LIVE IN A HOUSE THAT NEEDS CLEANING, SO DOES YOUR "BODY-HOUSE" NEED CLEANING. THE HOLY SPIRIT WANTS TO CLEAN UP WRONG THINKING AND ACTIONS.

THE HOUSE WITHOUT JESUS:

COLOR THE PICTURE.

86

NOW THAT THE HOLY SPIRIT LIVES IN YOU, HE IS GOING TO WANT TO CLEAN AND EVEN CHANGE SOME THINGS IN HIS HOUSE!

THIS TAKES TIME. BUT THE RESULT IS THAT YOU ARE MORE FREE AND MUCH HAPPIER AND THAT LIKE A NICE CLEAN HOUSE, YOU ARE MORE INVITING TO OTHERS. PEOPLE WILL WANT TO BE AROUND YOU, AND YOU CAN SHARE WITH THEM WHAT JESUS HAS DONE IN YOUR LIFE!

THE HOUSE WITH JESUS:

COLOR THE PICTURE.

87

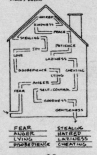

GO THROUGH THE HOUSE BELOW AND PICK UP THOSE THINGS THAT GOD WOULD CLEAN OUT. WRITE THEM IN THE BLANK SPACES BELOW.

HATRED
KINDNESS
STEALING PEACE
JOY PATIENCE
LOVE LAZINESS
DISOBEDIENCE CHEATING
LYING
ANGER SELF-CONTROL
FEAR GOODNESS
GENTLENESS

FEAR	STEALING
ANGER	HATRED
LYING	LAZINESS
DISOBEDIENCE	CHEATING

88

AGAIN, IT IS THE WORK OF THE HOLY SPIRIT THAT DOES THE CLEANING IN US. WE ONLY NEED US TO BE WILLING TO LET HIM DO THAT WORK.

GOD'S WORD GIVES US A PROMISE!

FIND THE UNDERLINED WORDS IN THE WORDSEARCH PUZZLE BELOW.

" BE CONFIDENT OF THIS, THAT HE WHO BEGAN A GOOD WORK IN YOU WILL CARRY IT ON TO THE FINISH UNTIL JESUS CHRIST COMES AGAIN."

PHILIPPIANS 1:6
(ILLUMINATED BIBLE)

89

PICTURE YOURSELF AS A SOLDIER! YOU ARE NOW A SOLDIER FOR JESUS CHRIST, AND HE GIVES US EVERYTHING WE NEED TO WIN THE BATTLE.

USE THE CODE CHART BELOW TO MATCH THE CODES WITH LETTERS. USE THE COLUMN GOING DOWN FIRST, THEN WRITE THE LETTERS IN THE BLANKS.

	1	2	3	4	5
5	A	F	K	P	U	Z
4	B	G	L	Q	V	
3	C	H	M	R	W	
2	D	I	N	S	X	
1	E	J	O	T	Y	

FINALLY, BE
STRONG IN THE
LORD AND IN HIS
MIGHTY POWER

CONT'D NEXT PAGE...

90

CONT'D FROM PREVIOUS PAGE.

PUT ON THE FULL
ARMOR OF GOD
SO THAT YOU CAN
TAKE YOUR STAND
AGAINST THE
DEVIL'S SCHEMES."

EPHESIANS 6:10-11

91

FIND THE UNDERLINED WORDS IN THE WORDSEARCH PUZZLE BELOW

" STAND FIRM THEN, WITH THE BELT OF TRUTH BUCKLED AROUND YOUR WAIST, WITH THE BREASTPLATE OF RIGHTEOUSNESS IN PLACE, AND WITH YOUR FEET FITTED WITH THE READINESS THAT COMES FROM THE GOSPEL OF PEACE. IN ADDITION TO ALL THIS, TAKE UP THE SHIELD OF FAITH, WITH WHICH YOU CAN EXTINGUISH ALL THE FLAMING ARROWS OF THE EVIL ONE. TAKE THE HELMET OF SALVATION AND THE SWORD OF THE SPIRIT, WHICH IS THE WORD OF GOD."

EPHESIANS 6:14-17

THIS IS THE FULL ARMOR OF GOD!

SHIELD	FITTED
WORD	TRUTH
HELMET	SWORD
BELT	GOSPEL
SALVATION	BREASTPLATE

92

FILL IN THE BLANKS.

SWORD OF THE SPIRIT

HELMET OF SALVATION

SHOES OF THE GOSPEL

BELT OF TRUTH

BREASTPLATE RIGHTEOUSNESS

SHIELD OF FAITH

THE FULL ARMOR OF GOD!

93

FINISH THE PICTURE.

DRAW OVER THE DOTTED LINES TO "DRESS" IN THE ARMOR OF GOD.

94

FIND YOUR WAY THROUGH THE BATTLEFIELD OF LIFE. WATCH OUT FOR TEMPTATION AND SIN!

END

95

DO YOU REMEMBER OUR THREE ENEMIES, THE WORLD, THE FLESH (OR HUMAN NATURE), AND THE DEVIL?

WE CALL THE BATTLE AGAINST THESE ENEMIES SPIRITUAL WARFARE.

GOD'S WORD HAS SOMETHING TO SAY ABOUT THIS WARFARE.

" FOR OUR STRUGGLE (OUR BATTLE) IS NOT AGAINST FLESH AND BLOOD, BUT AGAINST THE RULERS, AGAINST THE AUTHORITIES, AGAINST THE POWERS OF THIS DARK WORLD AND AGAINST THE SPIRITUAL FORCES OF EVIL IN THE HEAVENLY REALMS (OUR UNSEEN SPIRITUAL WORLD AROUND US)."

EPHESIANS 6:12

96

FLESH   RULERS
EVIL   BLOOD
WORLD   HEAVENLY
STRUGGLE   AUTHORITIES

97

NOW IT IS TIME TO START LIVING YOUR LIFE AS A CHILD OF GOD

THERE ARE MANY THINGS IN LIFE THAT CAN DISTRACT US, OR LEAD US AWAY, FROM JESUS.

WHAT DOES JESUS SAY WE SHOULD DO?

UNSCRAMBLE THE WORDS AND PUT THEM IN THE RIGHT PLACES IN THE VERSE BELOW.

" LET US _XFI_ OUR EYES ON JESUS, THE _RASHLO_ AND PERFECTER OF OUR _TAFIH_, WHO FOR THE _OYJ_ SET BEFORE HIM ENDURED THE _RSSCO_, SCORNING ITS _MSEHA_, AND SAT _OWNDN_ AT THE RIGHT _NZHA_ OF THE _HURCOE_ OF GOD."

—HEBREWS 12:2

" LET US _FIX_ OUR EYES ON JESUS, THE _AUTHOR_ AND PERFECTER OF OUR _FAITH_, WHO FOR THE _JOY_ SET BEFORE HIM ENDURED THE _CROSS_, SCORNING ITS _SHAME_, AND SAT _DOWN_ AT THE RIGHT _HAND_ OF THE _THRONE_ OF GOD."

98

WORDSEARCH

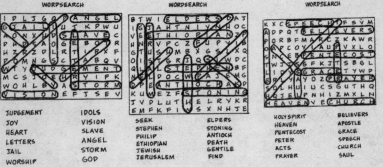

JUDGEMENT   IDOLS
JOY   VISION
HEART   SLAVE
LETTERS   ANGEL
JAIL   STORM
WORSHIP   GOD

99

WORDSEARCH

SEEK   ELDERS
STEPHEN   STONING
PHILIP   ANTIOCH
ETHIOPIAN   DEATH
JEWISH   GENTILE
JERUSALEM   FIND

100

WORDSEARCH

HOLY SPIRIT   BELIEVERS
HEAVEN   APOSTLE
PENTECOST   GRACE
PETER   SPEECH
ACTS   CHURCH
PRAYER   SAUL

101

WORDSEARCH

SALVATION   FAITH
BAPTISM   LIFE
WAY   TEMPTATION
HEALS   ETERNAL
TRUTH   SALT
LIGHT   LOVE

102

WORDSEARCH

HOLY   JOHN
SON   GOSPELS
LUKE   FATHER
MATTHEW   MARK
JAMES   TRINITY
GOD   JESUS

103

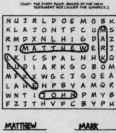

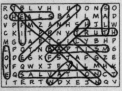

MATTHEW   MARK
LUKE   JOHN

104

WORDSEARCH

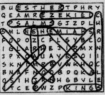

NEHEMIAH	ESTHER
ELISHA	EZRA
JOB	ISAIAH
SOLOMON	PROVERBS
PSALMS	CHRONICLES
KINGS	EZEKIEL

105

WORDSEARCH

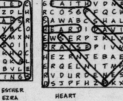

HEART	REFUGE
TRUTH	TRIALS
SINNER	SONG
PSALM	PRAISE
SHEPHERD	LORD
DAVID	FAITH

106

WORDSEARCH

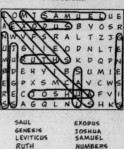

SAUL	EXODUS
GENESIS	JOSHUA
LEVITICUS	SAMUEL
RUTH	NUMBERS
JUDGES	MOSES

107

WORDSEARCH

JOSHUA	KING
JORDAN	LAWS
SIN	REST
COVENANT	HEBREWS
PROMISE	BUSH
STANDS	PHARAOH

108

GOD'S PROMISE

GOD HAS GIVEN ABRAM A NEW NAME THAT MEANS "FATHER OF NATIONS." HE HAS PROMISED ABRAM A SON.

CROSS OUT EVERY LETTER THAT APPEARS FOUR TIMES. THEN THE REMAINING LETTERS IN ORDER TO FIND HIS NEW NAME.

WHAT IS HIS NEW NAME ? __ABRAHAM__

109

WORDSEARCH

ADAM	ANGEL
CREATION	HOLY SPIRIT
SWORD	EARTH
TREE	EVE
SERPENT	TEMPTED
GARDEN	EDEN

110

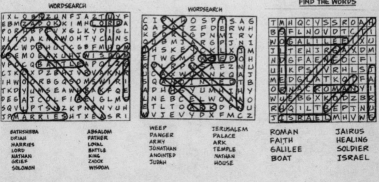

WORDSEARCH

BATHSHEBA	ABSALOM
URIAH	FATHER
MARRIES	LOYAL
LORD	BATTLE
NATHAN	KING
GRIEF	ZADOK
SOLOMON	WISDOM

111

WORDSEARCH

WEEP	JERUSALEM
DANGER	PALACE
ARMY	ARK
JONATHAN	TEMPLE
ANOINTED	NATHAN
JUDAH	HOUSE

112

FIND THE WORDS

ROMAN	JAIRUS
FAITH	HEALING
GALILEE	SOLDIER
BOAT	ISRAEL

113

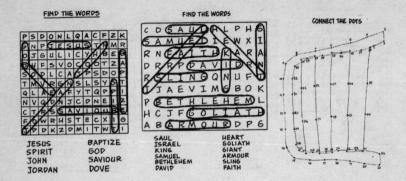

114

JESUS   BAPTIZE
SPIRIT   GOD
JOHN   SAVIOUR
JORDAN   DOVE

115

SAUL   HEART
ISRAEL   GOLIATH
KING   GIANT
SAMUEL   ARMOUR
BETHLEHEM   SLING
DAVID   FAITH

CONNECT THE DOTS

116

CONNECT THE DOTS

117

CONNECT THE DOTS

118

CONNECT THE DOTS

119

HELP BUILD THE TEMPLE
CONNECT THE DOTS

120

CONNECT THE DOTS
YOUNG DAVID WENT TO BATTLE AGAINST--?

UNSCRAMBLE:
HGTLIOA
G O L I A T H

121

CONNECT THE DOTS
JESUS, THE _LION_ OF JUDAH!

122

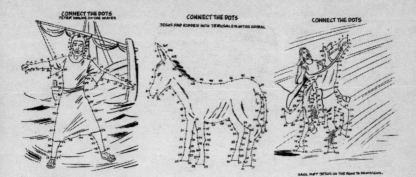

CONNECT THE DOTS
PETER WALKS ON THE WATER

CONNECT THE DOTS
JESUS HAD RIDDEN INTO JERUSALEM IN THIS ANIMAL

CONNECT THE DOTS

SAUL MET JESUS ON THE ROAD TO DAMASCUS.

123   124   125

THE TOWER OF BABEL

PEOPLE BUILT A HIGH TOWER TO PROVE HOW POWERFUL AND SMART THEY WERE—BUT GOD WAS NOT PLEASED.

UNSCRAMBLE THE WORDS AND PUT THEM IN PROPER ORDER TO FIND OUT WHAT GOD DID TO STOP THEM.

6. GESSAGLAN
L A N G U A G E S

5. IFFRRENTD
D I F F E R E N T

3. HTME
T H E M

2. DMAE
M A D E

1. ORG
G O D

4. EAPSK
S P E A K

G O D   M A D E   T H E M   S P E A K   D I F F E R E N T   L A N G U A G E S
1   2   3   4   5   6

128

WHAT IS A PSALM?

CROSS OUT EVERY LETTER THAT APPEARS FOUR TIMES IN THE PUZZLE. COPY THE REST OF THE LETTERS, IN ORDER, TO FIND THE ANSWER.

A D S P F E
F C P B O A
C N A C E O
P D F A G P

A PSALM IS A S O N G .

READ PSALM 23, THEN DRAW YOURSELF INTO THE PICTURE

141

SOLVE THE PUZZLE

J ESSE — DAVID'S FATHER
PHILISTINES — ISRAEL'S ENEMY
S AUL — KING OF ISRAEL
MUSIC — DAVID USES THIS TO COMFORT SAUL
S AMUEL — GOD'S PROPHET
ISRAEL — GOD'S NATION
S ONS OF JESSE — DAVID'S BROTHERS
LORD — GOD
GOLIATH — GIANT PHILISTINE
WAR — ISRAEL FIGHTS
DAVID — GOD'S NEW KING

WHAT DOES IT SAY?
J E S U S   I S   L O R D
1 2 3 4 5   6 7   8 9 10 11

142

WORD JUMBLE

OPH DOP   PTES OTOP   YRD BOY

HOW DAVID FLED FROM JERUSALEM

ON HIS ☐ ☐ ☐ ☐ ☐

143

JESUS AT THE TEMPLE

HOW OLD WAS JESUS THE FIRST TIME HE WENT TO THE TEMPLE? LOOK AT THE NUMBERED BRICKS, AND SOLVE THE EQUATION BELOW.

☐ + ☐ + ☐ + △ + ◇ + ☐ + ◇ + ☐ = 12

CIRCLE LUKE 2:41-52 TO MAKE SURE YOU HAVE THE RIGHT ANSWER.

145

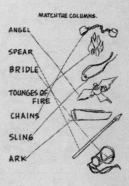

MATCH THE COLUMNS.

ANGEL
SPEAR
BRIDLE
TOUNGES OF FIRE
CHAINS
SLING
ARK

157

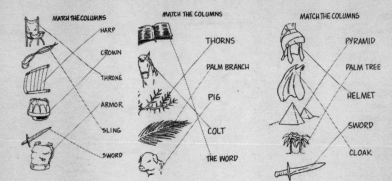

MATCH THE COLUMNS

HARP
CROWN
THRONE
ARMOR
SLING
SWORD

158

MATCH THE COLUMNS

THORNS
PALM BRANCH
PIG
COLT
THE WORD

159

MATCH THE COLUMNS

PYRAMID
PALM TREE
HELMET
SWORD
CLOAK

160

MATCH THE COLUMNS

STAFF
WATER JUG
FISHING BOAT
NET
SANDAL
ANGEL

161

PAUL'S MISSIONARY JOURNEY
HELP PAUL GET TO HIS DESTINATION OF ROME.

ANTIOCH
PHILIPPI
ATHENS
CORINTH
EPHESUS
THESSALONICA
ROME

162

JESUS WAS ARRESTED IN THE GARDEN OF GETHSEMANE. PETER TRIED TO GET AWAY FROM THE SOLDIERS. HELP HIM FIND HIS WAY OUT.

EXIT

163

ADD THE NUMBERS TO FIND OUT HOW MANY DAYS JESUS WAS IN THE DESERT.

5 . 5 . 2 . 3 . 2 . 5 . 2 . 3 . 3 . 2 . 5 . 4 =

164

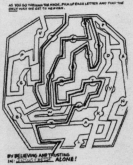

AS YOU GO THROUGH THE MAZE, PICK UP EACH LETTER AND FIND THE ONLY WAY WE GET TO HEAVEN.

BY BELIEVING AND TRUSTING IN: JESUS CHRIST ALONE!

165

MANY PATHS THAT LEAD NOWHERE - ONLY ONE SURE WAY. CAN YOU FIND IT?

FINISH

166

DANIEL AND THE ISRAELITES WERE TAKEN AS PRISONERS OF WAR TO BABYLON—A BIG AND BUSY CITY. HELP DANIEL FIND HIS NEW APARTMENT.

HELP THE ISRAELITES GET TO THE PROMISED LAND.

JOSEPH WAS SOLD AS A SLAVE BY HIS BROTHERS AND TAKEN TO EGYPT. HELP THE CARAVAN GET THROUGH THE DUNES AND AROUND THE BORDERS.

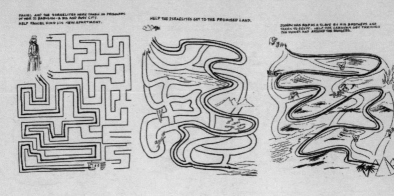

167

168

169

HELP DAVID ESCAPE SAUL

START

SAFETY

HELP DAVID GET OUT OF JERUSALEM

DAVID'S PALACE (START)

FINISH

HELP SAMUEL FIND THE SON OF JESSE THAT GOD HAS CHOSEN

JESSE'S SONS

DAVID

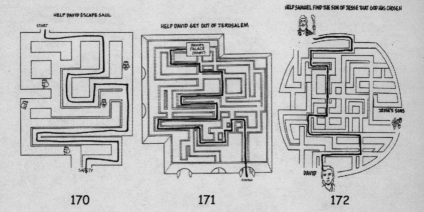

170

171

172

ON TO JERUSALEM!

START

FINISH

HELP JOSEPH, MARY, AND JESUS FIND THE WAY TO EGYPT

ABRAM IS MOVING
GOD HAS TOLD ABRAM TO MOVE BY FAITH. WHAT WILL HE TAKE WITH HIM?

COLOR ABRAM AND THE CORRECT ITEMS.

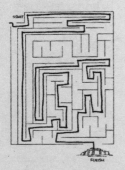

173

174

178

FIND THE DIFFERENCES

MOSES COMES DOWN THE MOUNTAIN WITH THE TEN COMMANDMENTS OF GOD. CIRCLE THE DIFFERENCES.

SNAKES IN THE DESERT

CIRCLE THE SEVEN DEADLY SNAKES.

FIND THE DIFFERENCES

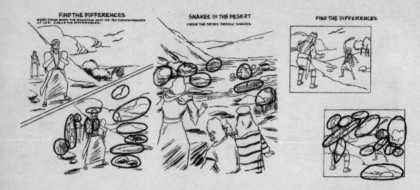

180

181

182

FIND THE DIFFERENCES

SOLOMON'S TEMPLE

FIND AT LEAST SIX DIFFERENCES IN THE TWO PICTURES BELOW!

JESUS IN THE MANGER

WHAT'S WRONG WITH THIS PICTURE?

ZACCHEUS, A WEALTHY TAX COLLECTOR, CLIMBED A TREE TO GET A BETTER LOOK AT JESUS. BUT, THIS IS A VERY STRANGE TREE. FIND AND CIRCLE WHAT DOESN'T BELONG.

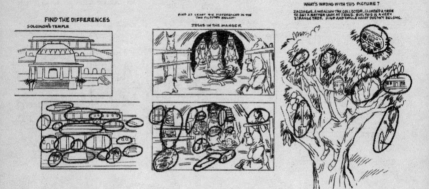

183

184

185

FIND ALL THE BREAD AND FISH

FIND THE DIFFERENCES

WHAT'S WRONG WITH THIS PICTURE?

JESUS HAD FIVE THOUSAND PEOPLE TO FEED. ONLY TWO OF THE ITEMS BELOW ARE WHAT HE USED TO WORK HIS MIRACLE. CIRCLE WHAT BELONGS.

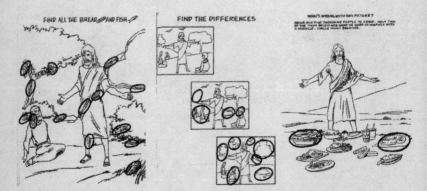

186

187

188

189

190

191

192

193

194

Check out these other

KIDS' BIBLE ACTIVITY BOOKS

from

Barbour Publishing

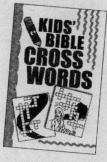

ISBN 1-59310-696-3

ISBN 1-59310-693-9

ISBN 1-59310-695-5

- 224 pages of fun
- Perfect for rainy days, car trips, and Sunday school classes
- Only $2.97 each

Available wherever books are sold.